PRAISE FOR
THE POWER OF DADHOOD

"Michael B. Smith's book, *The Power of Dadhood,* is the perfect gift for new fathers. It is especially important for the new father who did not benefit from being raised by an involved, caring, guiding father. This book offers a vision of what can be. It's easy to read, educational, motivational, and encouraging.

This book is full of common-sense parenting advice for a culture that lacks both common sense and fathering skills. Our society yearns for what is new and innovative, but in the area of fatherhood, it needs more of what Michael Smith is offering—age-old, tried-and-true wisdom about the oldest, most important human endeavor: raising kids."

—ANDY KERCKHOFF, author of *Critical Connection: A Practical Guide to Parenting Young Teens*

"Dadhood is a journey and sometimes can feel pretty lonely, but with Smith's wonderful book, *The Power of Dadhood*, one has a wise and helpful companion that makes you feel you are not alone. His book is full of helpful suggestions, insightful observations, and sage advice and is easy to read and understand. This is essential reading for any soon-to-be or new father but also to any woman who wants to support a man on his fatherhood journey. For the many who do not have healthy male mentors and role models, this book serves as an indispensable guide. I highly recommend this book."

—BARRY McINTOSH, Founder and Executive Director of Young Fathers of Santa Fe

"Michael Smith's own father was 'mostly absent,' which makes it even more impressive that Michael was not only a present and nurturing dad for his own kids, but also saw the role as important and fulfilling enough that he took the time to put his experiences and his wisdom into a book to benefit other fathers. If there is one thing that could save our culture and our society, it would be more present and proactive 'dadhood' by fathers throughout America!"

—RICHARD EYRE, *New York Times* #1 bestselling author of *Teaching Your Children Values*, *The Turning* (and father of nine)

"Research concludes that a youth's success in life falls largely on the shoulders of his father. In fact, a child is 90 percent more likely to successfully attend college if his father is intentionally involved in his/her life, especially school life. Mike Smith understands the critical need of a father's contribution to his children's well-being and his book is a critical tool for mentoring men to shoulder that burden. If read and applied, it will almost guarantee a 'slam dunk' success for their children. Mike's heartfelt desire to encourage men to want more for their children is compelling. No man wants 'father absence' to define him. Mike's work helps us on the road to making this world the place it should be for young children."

—LAURIE WENZEL, Director of Early Childhood Education, Pattonville School District, Professor of Early Childhood Education, Maryville University

"*The Power of Dadhood* is a concise, easy-to-read book on an important and timely topic. It includes a wealth of information, ranging from the impact fathers have on their children to specific ways to become better parents. It should be required reading for all fathers."

—MARGARET ALBRECHT, Retired Parent Educator with the Parents as Teachers program, Former Curriculum Writer, Parents as Teachers National Office

The Power of Dadhood will encourage men to *father* as themselves with the knowledge that they are vitally important to the futures of their children. Michael Byron Smith discusses the implications of a fatherless home, the challenges of parenting, and the hierarchy of fathers. There are absent fathers, present yet uninvolved fathers, authoritative fathers, loving fathers, teaching fathers, and more. Any man, through this book, can assess himself, see where he stands, and make choices to become a real Dad—and find the *Power of Dadhood*!

"My dad, he's thinking of me."
(See quote in upper right corner.)

My son's perception of his dad when he attended preschool. It is a peek inside the mind of a child, revealing a need all children have and deserve.

FAMILIUS

Familius books are available at special discounts for bulk purchases for sales promotions or for family, or corporate use. Special editions, including personalized covers, excerpts of existing books, or books with corporate logos, can be created in large quantities for special needs. For more information, contact Premium Sales at 559-876-2170 or email specialmarkets@familius.com.

Library of Congress Catalog-in-Publication Data

2015930672

Paperback ISBN 978-1-939629-66-1
Hardcover ISBN 978-1-942672-81-4
Ebook ISBN 978-1-942672-08-1

Printed in the United States of America

Edited by Caroline Bliss Larsen
Cover design by David Miles
Book design by Maggie Wickes

10 9 8 7 6 5 4 3 2 1

First Edition

THE POWER OF
DADHOOD

HOW TO BECOME
THE FATHER
YOUR CHILD NEEDS

FAMILIUS

MICHAEL BYRON SMITH

This book is dedicated to fathers everywhere and to all children who are in need of a father's love, attention, and support.

It is also dedicated with love to my wife, my children, and my grandchildren, without whom I would have no credibility.

WHAT EVERY DAD SHOULD TEACH
HIS CHILDREN

The joy of being involved in life.

The ability to generate happiness from within.

A deep, genuine kindness toward others.

Guiding principles that will lead them to a life of integrity.

A strong desire to help others and serve without need for recognition.

Resilience, becoming even stronger in the face of challenge.

A love and appreciation for the simple things in life and the awareness to notice them.

The recognition that they alone choose how to react to any given situation.

The talent to choose well.

—Michael Byron Smith

ACKNOWLEDGMENTS

I would like to thank my family for being so encouraging and patient over the many years I worked on this book. I want to thank my mom for working so hard to raise me, my brothers, and my sisters without the help of my father. I want to thank my daughter April McLellan, whose talent in writing and journalism taught me how to organize a jumble of thoughts into something readable. She believed in me and this project and gave me the voice I needed. I want to thank my wife, Kathy, for sharing her professional insight and knowledge of the issues of single teen mothers and how children learn from both parents. She was always supportive of my time away writing and researching in cafés and libraries, and she took on much of the duties at home. My daughter Rachel and son Michael were constant inspirations to me through their successes, kindness, and love of life.

I owe much to Nancy Robertson Cook, who reviewed my first draft and gave me many ideas and tons of encouragement. Without the validation of Dr. Sally Gafford, I would not have dared to go forth on my own. Her guidance and words of support as a family therapist were vital in validating my thoughts about fatherhood. I want to also thank Randy Stone, a neighbor, friend, and fellow father, for looking at this book through the eyes of a dad and making valued contributions and support. Thanks to my many friends who listened to my stories, frustrations, and complaints through the years. Also thanks to Maggie Lichtenberg who, as a publishing coach, taught me so much and provided me invaluable contacts and lasting lessons I will never forget. And lastly, a lasting thanks to editors Jeff Braucher and especially Caroline Bliss Larsen, whose suggestions and insightful questions helped to clarify my thoughts and message.

CONTENTS

ABOUT THIS BOOK

This is a mentoring book. It mentors men who are fathers, especially young fathers, and fathers-to-be. Mentors are not necessarily experts, but they've been there before. They can give you some tips on what works and what doesn't work.

While some men thrive naturally as fathers, there are too many who don't, and the results can be disastrous. We must not judge these men because we don't know what they've been through, how they were raised, or how they see things as a unique personality. But they could use a mentor, especially if their father was not there for them.

As I was growing up, I felt the need for a dad in my life and the lives of my siblings. Our father was often absent or unreachable, whether away from home or in the next room.

At an early age, I became determined to create myself as a real dad—one who provides his children with love, interaction, mentoring, and discipline—not a father who contributes only DNA.

I have gathered in this book my experiences and thoughts, the thoughts of others, and the personal stories of friends and family so that men young or not so young can move themselves beyond fatherhood to the irreplaceable state of Dadhood.

Throughout this book, I capitalize the D in Dad to emphasize the difference between merely being a biological father and achieving the ideal of being a wonderful, loving, and involved Dad.

Please be aware that it is NEVER too late to become a capital D Dad, and that your relationship with your kids will be better, stronger, and healthier when you show you care, whether your kids are infants, children, teenagers, or adults.

As you travel the road from fatherhood to Dadhood through the pages of this book, I will guide you to stop along the way and assess where you are. It's not a matter of flying a supersonic jet to travel from fatherhood to the state of Dad. It is a steady, intentional, mile-by-mile, where-the-rubber-meets-the-road process that can move any man from any background to the consequential and fulfilling state of Dadhood (and Granddadhood). And when you take this road, you are making society better, one child at a time.

FOREWORD

The Power of Dadhood is a book for fathers. It may be for a young man who finds himself in a situation he has never really comprehended. It may be for a busy father who is having difficulty fulfilling his role and has nowhere to turn. It could even be for the father who is away too much or does not feel comfortable in his own home. Then again, it could be for responsible fathers who just want to be better Dads.

Michael Smith witnessed firsthand the consequences of not having a caring father in the home. He was determined not to repeat the mistakes of his father, mistakes that can take generations from which to recover. Unlike most, he escaped the trap of a disadvantaged youth, which allowed him to be a better father to his children.

As a family therapist, I see people every day suffering from the lack of fatherly attention. The symptoms are many, but the cause is common to all those whose fathers were absent, distant, or cruel. Smith talks directly to fathers, man to man, giving encouragement, advice, and the knowledge that they are crucial in their children's lives.

I endorse the lessons and advice in Smith's book. The evidence of the need for better fathering is clearly laid out. The simplicity of the basic acts of fatherhood is clearly stated. And the ways to become an even better father are there for those who are already good fathers. But the challenges of being a good father cannot be ignored, and they are also addressed.

Michael Smith wanted to "be there" for his children. His simple advice will help you be there for your kids and perform basic acts of love that create a legacy benefiting not only your children, but their children and society as a whole.

—SALLY H. GAFFORD, PhD, Family Therapy

INTRODUCTION

"The hunger for love is much more difficult to remove than the hunger for bread."

—Mother Teresa

No man is a failure who has helped a child, especially his own. The greatest single gift a man can give his children is his attention. It seems so simple, but somehow it is lost in its simplicity. There is no excuse for not trying your best to be a good father. There are reasons, obstacles, and hardships, but no excuses.

Most would agree that fatherhood does not come as naturally as motherhood. I have little doubt that a woman is more likely to pick up this book than a man, even though it is targeted for men. We want to be attentive, caring fathers for the most part, and while not difficult intellectually, parenting for men is not necessarily intuitive either. The simplest of tasks appear difficult when we have no idea where to start. Swimming is not particularly difficult, but without some basic lessons, we could easily drown. We men need help with fathering before we drown not only ourselves, but also our children.

Whereas most occupations require some education or previous experience, you are not required to be educated in parenting before you become a dad. As a lawyer, bomber pilot, carpenter, or truck driver, you have had lots of training, advice, mentoring, and guidance in your field. But as a father, you may have to seek knowledge and advice on your own.

To help meet that need, this book offers a grassroots discussion by an everyday father regarding the importance and issues of being a father. My thoughts and suggestions on fatherhood may be of use to you, or you may disagree. But if you have cracked open this book, you want to be a good father, and that alone will make you one of the better fathers on earth. Stimulating thought and discussion about being a better father can only help us and our children. Incompetent fathering, and subsequently its dire consequences, must be exposed and resolved.

I learned so much from my father. I learned from him that I needed to get an education. I learned that people would judge me by my actions and react to me according to my attitude. I learned the importance of reliability and trust. These things I learned from him because he demonstrated how difficult life can be without them.

Unfortunately, I also saw how dependence on alcohol and drugs could steal my father's charm and waste his intelligence. Yes, I learned quite a bit about life from my father, but what I didn't learn was difficult to pick up on my own. Among those lessons missed early on were simple skills and pleasures of standing up straight, manners, confidence, physical competition, love of reading, and being comfortable in my own skin. Yes, my dad graduated from the School of Hard Knocks, but it is not exactly in the Ivy League of Childhood Mentoring. Too easy to get accepted into, his school lacked standards for graduation.

Why did I write this book?

I am the oldest of six children of an undereducated mother and a mostly absent father. With the turmoil in my family, we moved often, and I went to no less than thirty-five schools. Unfortunately, I was the only one in our family who graduated from high school, not to mention college. Fortunately, I learned how to set goals, which brought me out of a chaotic situation that many fail to escape. I studied hard, received an academic scholarship to college, and joined the Air Force as an officer. I married at age twenty-five after dating my wife for six years. I couldn't wait to be a father, and I wanted to be a good one.

My wife was unquestionably the main caretaker of our children. She put her career on hold for twenty years while I was the breadwinner. But I did spend quality time with my children and was a very present factor in their lives. Had my brothers and sisters had a loving and caring father, their lives would no doubt have been positively and significantly impacted. So would have mine.

Almost all of society's ills can be traced to people whose family lives were in turmoil. Often the turmoil started with an absent or uncaring father. What if there were a simple, plain-English book that addressed issues of fatherhood for men without positive role models? Where could a single mother direct her son when he has questions about becoming a father? How could the fatherless cycle be broken?

I wrote this book to help fathers, mothers, and children as individuals, with the hope that society as a whole will also benefit by the incremental improvement in people's lives. If just one father and child is helped by this book, I will feel greatly rewarded.

HOW TO USE THE ROAD MAP

As a summary for each chapter and as a tool for later review, I've included a "road map." You can unfold this map at any time to get your bearings when you are lost in the world of Dadhood.

Start: A simple but important point to understand before you continue on your journey.

Major Highway: This is a major theme of the chapter. You must become very familiar with this thoroughfare.

On the Open Road: Something to think about regarding this chapter. Not unlike a side trip along the way.

[Chapter number, i.e. First, Second] Stop: This is the main point of this leg of the trip. Why you are here?

I sincerely hope you have a successful journey on your trip through Dadhood!

THE
IMPLICATIONS OF
FATHERHOOD

CHAPTER 1

THE POWER OF FATHERHOOD

"Most American children suffer too much mother and too little father."

—Gloria Steinem

BLUE SKIES ARE JUST ABOVE THOSE CLOUDS

It was a dreary, chilly day with heavy fog and drenching rain, just like the day before. My little daughter walked up to where I was sitting and, because she was just the right height, lifted her chin and laid it on my knee. I remember stroking her hair, her head full of curly ringlets. As I bent to meet her eyes, I noticed they were half-moons, facing down toward her chubby cheeks.

Feeling the weight of such a gloomy atmosphere, she said, "Daddy, I'm tired of the rain. I wish it would go away."

I knew what she meant, because the days and days of rain were making me feel a little down myself. Trying to lift our spirits a bit and help her see things differently, I drew upon my experience as a pilot.

"You know, just above those clouds, not very far away, are bright-blue, crystal-clear skies."

"But, Daddy," she moaned. "We can't see the sky. All we see are yucky clouds and rain!"

"That's true. But knowing that sunshine and blue skies are near, just above those clouds, helps. It's true, we can't see the bright-blue sky now, but I promise you, it is there, and it's very close. And when you see it again, the sun will be shining brighter, in even bluer skies and on even greener pastures."

Knowing my daughter, I knew another challenge was coming. She wanted so much to be convinced. She wanted so much to be comforted.

"But what if it's nighttime?" she asked.

"Then you have the stars! Sunshine, stars, clear skies . . . they're all right behind the clouds," I said, hoping I'd finally won the debate. Those thoughts made her smile, and she went about her way with a little more bounce in her short little steps.

So why do I bring up this simple story of a father comforting his daughter? It reveals how simple it can be to be an effective dad—or Dad, with a capital D, as we'll call all great dads throughout this book. The importance of just being there with your children is never to be underestimated. By being there, talking together, you are connecting. Being there shows caring and creates quiet moments for teaching, encouragement, and love. Your simple presence and those quiet conversations, because of who you are and how impressionable they are, will have leverage beyond most other experiences and will be life-changing for both you and your children.

Being there sets the stage for creating strong footings in your relationship with your children, even if they don't consciously remember these specific moments. What is important does not have much to do with the story itself. The impact is in the sincerity and the interplay that tells your child that you are there to help and watch over them.

Just like the blue sky when obscured by rain clouds, your powerful, positive influence can be obscured by indifference or ignorance. Or, you can choose to *be* the blue skies behind the rain clouds, offering your presence, your time, your unconditional love.

MEN AS FATHERS

"I cannot think of any need in childhood as strong as the need for a father's protection."
—Sigmund Freud

There are too many men who procreate but never earn the title of "Dad." The word *father* to them is a label, not a commitment. They don't want the responsibility of a child, and they blame others for their predicament.

There are other men who meet their parental responsibilities by providing food, clothing, shelter, and discipline. They do this robotically without much emotion or interplay.

> ### DAD TIP:
> *There are too many men who procreate but never earn the title of "Dad." The word father to them is a label, not a commitment. Fatherhood is a never-ending series of loving, caring actions, not one single act.*

There are others still who provide the basics while also creating a warm, loving atmosphere. Likely, most fathers fall into this category. However, at the top of the pyramid are those men who not only provide for their children within a loving atmosphere, but also nurture, praise, and teach their children—throughout their lives. These men are heroes to their children and are among the most stalwart pillars of our society. Their contributions are often hidden. We do not conceive of what may have happened without them, and they are rarely celebrated. But statistically, we can and will see what loving, nurturing fathers have done and will continue to do for both children and our society.

WHAT IT TAKES TO BE A REAL DAD

A Dad does *not* need to be handsome, strong, athletic, macho, rich, eloquent, college educated, or even married to the child's mother, as is often the situation. Although many men want to be these things, such characteristics don't make a man a Man or a father a Dad.

A Dad *does* need to be loving, available, caring, interested, and involved, as well as a nurturing teacher, disciplinarian, coach, cheerleader, and so much more.

Many men would like to be handsome, rich, eloquent, and more, as would I, but these traits should never come as a substitute for qualities that make them real Dads. We've all known men who were shams, showing a jovial and interested face to the world but a sullen, unengaged, and even surly face to his family. The sham father is just a house of cards, big on appearances but otherwise sorely lacking. The real Dad has a solid foundation as a leader and mentor—with a greater likelihood of entering that zone of being a wonderful Dad.

I say this to my fellow men: you don't create children to fulfill your own vision, but you do create opportunities for them to discover themselves so they can become happy and at ease with themselves.

Being a father is not a competition. It constitutes selfless, loving acts toward other human beings—human beings that you and their mother have brought into this world.

THE POSITIVE IMPACTS OF GOOD FATHERING

I contend, without any hesitation, that if every father in this country, working cooperatively with a positive, responsible mother, were to consider and successfully apply responsible parenting principles and values:

- incidents of crime and hate would plummet remarkably.
- personal success and general happiness would increase.
- mental health issues would be greatly reduced.

But the seventeen-year-old father who can barely take care of himself, or the new thirty-two-year-old father who has lived a mostly selfish single life, or the businessman who has been too busy to really pay attention to his kids—these men and other fathers don't necessarily need to concern themselves with the greater societal good so much as they need to make honest efforts at being the best fathers they can be. Society will then take care of itself.

DAD TIP:

Involved Dads can change not only the lives of their children but also the course of our nation. A Dad's most important act is making an honest effort at being the best father he can be to his children.

So whether these claims of a better society are bold or obvious, we know that improving the participation and skills of all fathers will certainly be good for our children. This is our goal. This is the potential of the power of fatherhood.

WHAT A REAL FATHER KNOWS

How does a father teach his children the lessons needed to deal with life, everyday living, and the world? First of all, it helps if he is aware of and accepts these important aspects of fathering:

- Neither he nor any other father knows everything or ever will.
- His mistakes must not discourage him.
- His actions are being observed.
- He must be consistent, loving, sincere, and available.
- Humor will be an ally.

- His children must experience struggle (supervised, if possible) to learn and grow.
- Every child is unique and learns differently and at a different pace.

With this knowledge as a basis, a man can follow through with his responsibilities as a father and successfully perform the things that only a father can do.

WHAT ONLY A FATHER CAN DO FOR A SON

- A boy can learn to be a man, but only a father can teach the right way—with love and without "initiations" or competition.
- Only a father can counteract the unrealistic demands of false masculinity (machismo).
- A father's stern look or serious tone can stop an out-of-control son before it's too late.
- A boy can play catch with a friend, but there's nothing like playing catch with Dad.
- Only a father recognizes when a son needs to establish his masculine identity, and only a father knows how to provide and teach it.
- A firm handshake, a bear hug, an approving nod, a disapproving stare—each is best done by a father. Of course a mother can do these too, but a boy might be more likely to respond to these things from his father.

WHAT ONLY A FATHER CAN DO FOR A DAUGHTER

- Of course, only a father can take his daughter to a father-daughter dance.
- Only a father can best make his daughter feel safe from harm.
- Only a father's pride in his daughter can make her feel special in ways different from the pride of her mother.

- Only a father can best demonstrate to his daughter how she ought to be treated by a man.
- A daughter can be loved by another man, but never in the same way as her father loves her.

WHAT ONLY A FATHER CAN DO, IN GENERAL

- Only a father can love his children as deeply as their mother does.
- Only a father can provide the necessary diversion from and for the mother.
- Usually it is the father who throws his babies in the air and carries them on his shoulders. He is the one who clowns around with his kids and balances brooms on his chin.
- Only a father can make you embarrassed and proud at the same time.
- Only a father, with a good mother, can help society reduce violence, alleviate anger, ease anxiety, and promote the family—one child at a time. The roots of society's problems are often caused by the fatherlessness of young boys and girls. Little in society can solve the resulting social violence, drug use, out-of-wedlock births, psychological problems, and character flaws—nothing except an involved, caring, mentoring, parental team in every family.
- Children can be financially supported through public agencies or the kindness of others. But this can make children (old enough to know what's going on) feel ashamed and embarrassed. Some families are supported financially by the mother alone, but without the help of a father, she will have to endure financial and parental challenges alone.

When a man recognizes these points, he is either energized or frightened. If energized, he accepts his role and the vital impacts he can make. If frightened, he may not be ready to be a Dad and should be more responsible in his choices regarding fatherhood.

Should we expect all men to be good fathers? Should all men even be fathers?

DAD TIP:

Dads don't have to be perfect; it's not an all-or-nothing deal. But Dads do need to be consistent, loving, sincere, and available. Being a Dad means being there and being engaged with your child.

A CRY FOR LOVE AND COMFORT

A Dad's role in love and comfort is to complement the mother's. Children can have the most wonderful, loving mother in the world yet still feel incomplete without the love of their father. This is because a father fulfills different needs for their children. The differences in those needs could be personality driven, gender driven, or driven by an otherwise unexplainable connection. Your children are automatically filled by your love. A child's need for fatherly love is universally underestimated and without bounds.

I discovered on an Internet forum a beautiful yet heart-wrenching example of a young woman's desire for the attention of her father. Written by a girl from Nigeria with the username Princess, this excerpt is in her own words. Spelling has been normalized, and minimal punctuation and capitalization have been added for clarity:

> Some days I feel like life is not too much without getting love from fathers, but many of us can relate to [a] situation like this. Deep inside I feel hurt even though I am mad at him, but I know that I need love, lots of love from a father. My heart cries every time I see people or kids my age with their dads having so much fun. I wish that was me. I guess some people just aren't meant to have what others have. Before I sleep I pray to God to give me that love of a father I wanted all my life for about three years now, but I guess I am

not that lucky. Even though it's hurt me a lot not having good relationship with him, I still wish that he will come and love me just as a father [is] supposed to love his kid. This is what I pray to God for:

Lord have mercy upon my father.

I am pretty sure he doesn't mean to hurt me.

Give him the heart to love me.

Forgive him and make him a new person again.

I want him to show me love.

Deep inside he has killed my spirit to love men.

He made me think that all men are like that.

God, even though he hurt me, I have forgiven him.

All [I] am asking you to do is to help him realize that you are God

And surrender himself to you.

Thank you Lord, amen.

I know there [are] many out there that can relate to me, but all [I] am asking y'all to do for me is to help me pray for my father. Help me pray for God to forgive him. I need a fatherly love. I want a fatherly love. I will be happy again if there is peace between me and him.

She presents her need simply and eloquently. Nothing I could add would make her need more evident. I simply repeat: *a child's need for fatherly love is universally underestimated and without bounds.*

DADS ARE AVAILABLE

Providing love and comfort is not defined in any one way. It can be as simple as a touch or a wink, as complicated as family therapy, or as thoughtful as a long-distance phone call. He simply needs to be available.

When my kids were of preschool age, my wife would dress them and comb their hair most of the time. I would hold them in my lap or play with them. I had the easy job but nevertheless an important one. Now could these roles be reversed? Of course! The mother and father must be flexible. Look for opportunities to fill the gap between parental roles. Be a team. There is no one role a father must fill, but he must fill *some* role that includes being available when the children need him.

A simple act of caring from her father, simply being available, would have made a world of difference in the Nigerian woman's life. To children, young or grown, a father's support enables them to take risks. You are their safety net because you are on their side, constantly and enthusiastically. If they succeed, you will be there to celebrate. If they fail, you will be there to recognize their efforts and to encourage them to try again. A hug or a pat on the back is a powerful thing, especially when it's from your Dad.

DAD TIP:
Showing your children that you care makes a world of difference in their lives. A hug or a pat on the back is a powerful thing, especially when it's from their Dad. Demonstrating that you do not care leaves a void that can never be filled.

CHILDREN LEARN FROM THEIR DADS DIFFERENTLY

What a father does to prepare his children for the challenges of life will likely be different from their mother's approach.

Roles are sometimes stereotyped. We often think of mothers as the main caregivers (brushing teeth, ensuring clean underwear), while fathers are generally more like the finishers, helping mom with these chores while often exposing the children to new and different experiences. A simple example is roughhousing. Wrestling around with your children is a way to subtly teach them the limits of aggression and how to control it, and to respect strength, power, and authority (NCPFCE).

Fathers and mothers complement each other and should support each other. Nothing says that traditional gender roles can't be reversed, and certainly in today's society they are often blurred. Having two caring adults raise their children allows them to supplement each other in teaching and reinforcing lessons in life and love.

THE PYRAMID OF DADHOOD

Fathering styles can range from being totally out of the picture to being a controlling tyrant. We want a father to be around, but not in the way. We want him to be loving, but not overprotective. We want to learn from him, but not if he's teaching a lack of values and self-respect.

So to be an effective father means to understand the need for balance and to have solid principles. That's not too much to ask, but it is a tough assignment to deliver because the father has to be present, physically and emotionally, while also providing for his family.

The Pyramid of Dadhood shows a hierarchy of traits needed for effective fathering. The foundation of the pyramid is for a father to be present in a child's life, a necessary place to start and an immediate and immeasurable benefit to all involved.

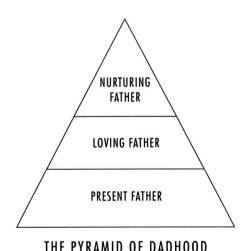

THE PYRAMID OF DADHOOD

At the next level of the pyramid, a father expresses love for his children and provides for their safety and comfort. When he achieves or naturally acts from this level, it is a colossal benefit to his children and lays the foundation for the pyramid's pinnacle, where the father teaches, nurtures, and prepares his children for life. This hierarchy will be discussed in detail in future chapters.

Challenges do exist within each step and among all involved. None of this responsibility comes easily. If it did, the need for more fathers actually fathering would not be so great.

The missing father does not act within this pyramid. We can only discuss why he may be absent and the implications of his absence as they impact his children and our society, which we will do in chapter 2.

YOUR ROAD MAP: CHAPTER 1

Start: Be there with and for your children.

Major Highway: Talk with your children. Listen to what they have to say. Teach them what you have learned from living your life thus far. Talk together about anything. Just be there.

On the Open Road: Imagine how our culture could improve if more fathers were involved with their kids. You can't make other men be involved, but you can make a difference in your own children's lives by striving to love and comfort them. You can be an example to other dads.

First Stop: Think about where you are in the Pyramid of Dadhood. What could you do to move up a level? When you get to the top level, remember this: There are unending levels of nurturing and teaching. You can always find ways to adjust and expand.

SAVIDA

THIS GARMENT IS UNIQUE IN COLOUR. ACHIEVED
THROUGH A SPECIAL DYEING PROCESS. INTIALLY
COLOUR MAY RUB OFF WHILE WEARING AND
WASHING. THIS DOES NOT DIMINISH THE QUALITY OF
THE GARMENT. BUT IS CHARACTERISTIC OF THE
PLANT DERIVED INDIGO WE THEREFORE RECOMMEND
WASHING GARMENT SEPARATELY AND WITHOUT
BLEACHING AGENTS TO RETAIN THE
ORIGINAL APPEARANCE.

ESTA PRENDA TIENE UN COLOR UNICO. LOGRADO
A TRAVES DE UN ESPECIAL PROCESO DE TINTADO
INICIALMENTE EL COLOR PODRIA
DECOLORARSE POR EL USO Y LOS LAVADOS.
ESTO NO DISMINUYE LA CALIDAD DELA PRENDA.
SI NO GUE ES UNA CARACTERISTICA DE ESTA PLANTA
DERIVADA DEL INDIGO. RECOMENDAMOS LAVA
ESTA PRENDA SEPARADAMENTE Y SINS LEJIAS
PARA MANTENER EL ESPECTO ORIGINAL

CHAPTER 2

THE ABSENT FATHER

"It is easier for a father to have children than for children to have a real father."

—Pope John XXIII

FATHERLESS TRENDS ARE GROWING

It takes a father's sperm and a mother's egg to bring a child into the world. Love is not required. But it takes a father's love and a mother's love to properly raise a child. While the joining of sperm and egg always takes place when a child is conceived, the joining of parents in raising their child doesn't take place often enough.

Despite the obvious benefits of having a good father in the home, the trend of fatherless homes is growing. In 2011, forty-one percent of women who gave birth were unwed, up from five percent in 1960. Readily available statistics tell us that when a mother and father are not married, within five years almost all the fathers of these children are gone—if not long before.

Many of these men would remain in their children's lives if they were given some encouragement, if they knew how important they were, and if they had some mentoring.

As dads, we were all young boys once, dependent upon and affected by others. No doubt our parents had the most potential to mold us, but *both* parents needed to be involved for our highest benefit. Though not necessarily a bad thing, often the mother is predominantly involved in childcare, especially in the first year. But fathers must also play a role to ensure a balanced childhood.

The impact of an absent father is far from optimal. But let's face it, father absence can occur even if he is in the home. The role your father played or didn't play in your childhood will have much to do with the kind of father you will, or could, become.

You have the ability to choose—you can become a great Dad, even if you did not have one in your life when you were a child. But it takes work, and it takes dedication.

WHAT IS HAPPENING?

Many fathers are wonderful, but too many are not. Too many have abandoned their children and the children's mother, either physically or emotionally. Emotional abandonment can be slow and destructive to a relationship, identifiable when fathers are distant, uninvolved, ineffective, irresponsible, and unrepentant for their actions. Fearing physical abandonment, the wives or partners of these men, in many instances, have not expressed their objection to such behaviors. Their silence only serves to keep their partners centered only on themselves.

Women have often struggled to effectively raise their children without the help of the childrens' father, striving to overcome the deficiencies of fatherlessness. But regardless of the brave and tireless actions of the mothers of this world, only with a mother *and* father can a child's life be truly whole. Fatherless children can be happy, or think they are, but they will have missed significant lessons and experiences.

> **DAD TIP:**
> *It takes dedication to be involved. Too many fathers are absent from their children's lives. And let's face it, men can be present in the home, but be absent from family relationships. Be involved!*

WHY SOME THINK FATHERS ARE UNNECESSARY

> *"The place of the father in the modern suburban family is a very small one, particularly if he plays golf."*
> —Bertrand Russell

You may disagree with me on the importance of fathers. Many people do, including some supposed experts on parenting. Those who have a jaded view of the need for involved fathers probably think of those described by Bertrand Russell.

Your *place* in the modern family is as small or as large as you make it. But your *impact* is undeniably large, and it's your choice what kind of impact you want to make.

> **DAD TIP:**
> *Think about your relationship with each of your children. What is your place in each child's life? And the more important question is: what impact are you choosing to make on your child's life?*

MORE OPINIONS: A DISTURBING TREND

To read examples of an American trend toward the "accepted absent father," see David Blankenhorn's chapter, "The Unnecessary Father," in his book, *Fatherless America: Confronting Our Most Urgent Social Problem*. *Fatherless America* details how the social role of fathers has been diminished and devalued.

Blankenhorn writes:

> According to many experts, some mothers, and certain aspects of society, fathers are unnecessary. A father's presence is appreciated but not required in a family. His role is overemphasized while the role of other adults is underemphasized. He is easily replaced by other male role models. . . .
>
> Experts speak of having one or both parents present as making little difference in the socialization of children. They say that there are positives to being a single parent. That children don't need a father to develop normally. That fathers are superfluous. . . .
>
> One expert states we should rid studies of the "nuclear family bias" because family structure in and of itself has little to do with the development of children. Some mothers don't want the men who are their children's father getting in the way. They like having better control of their children without having another parent (third party) involved.

Like Blankenhorn, I am disappointed to see that some of these "experts" hold such a narrow view of the value of fatherhood.

THE INFLUENCE OF MEDIA AND CELEBRITIES

The media can shape society's views of fatherhood. Both written and electronic media shape people's opinions in subtle ways. The Internet plays a huge role through social media and blogs—even through sites you (or your children) frequently visit. The media, including the Internet, can play a positive role or a negative one, depending on what people take as fact, and whether or not they explore other views. On television today, the role of unmarried mothers as the stars on both afternoon and prime time TV is common, and they often are portrayed as not wanting or needing a spouse in their lives.

Nick at Nite and TV Land are popular channels for revisiting shows from the 60s, 70s, and 80s—and even some new shows produced today. It's sad that few TV shows since the 1960s show fathers in a positive light. In too many shows (not all, but many), fathers through the decades are progressively shown more to be buffoons, absent, uninvolved, clueless, or cruel.

Prime time television explores social mores of the day. *Murphy Brown* was a TV series that broke many barriers in the late 1980s and 90s. One portion of the series's progression was championing a woman choosing to have and raise a baby on her own. While giving pride and hope to single mothers—a good thing—another consequence was placing a tacit stamp of approval on a fatherless upbringing.

For nine seasons from 1996 to 2005, *Everybody Loves Raymond* portrayed Raymond as a good guy, but also as a selfish man who was rarely involved in the lives of his children—a father present but often unengaged.

Today, one of the most popular TV shows is *Two and a Half Men*. This show does portray a present father, to be sure. But the many social situations involved in the show don't make it easy for Alan to continually show his son, Jake, the best models of manhood.

Other TV fathers throughout the years have simply been portrayed as bumbling idiots—think of Homer Simpson. But take heart; bumbling idiots can still be effective fathers. They just have to be loving and involved.

One of the results of our children's—or our own—idolization of television stars, movie stars, and sports heroes provides another subtle, underlying hint at the responsibility of fatherhood. Some who are idolized have children out of wedlock, as do people across other segments of society. Yet they are in the public eye, followed closely by the media, and are often looked up to as examples. By their actions, some of them are showing their fans, and more importantly their younger fans, that it is okay to be a mother in a fatherless house, or a father who ends his involvement when the seed is sown.

Personalities in sports and entertainment have the tremendous advantage of a public stage upon which to present their views, morals, or philosophies. Sadly, these are often at odds with the positive aspects of living within a nuclear family or an arrangement where the father is engaged and involved.

Often in news stories or movie and TV scripts, childcare payments from fathers seem more important and more persistently pursued than paternal childcare itself. Sure, some families may be better off without certain types of fathers, such as abusive or alcoholic fathers. Some fathers have differing views of parenting from mothers, which can make child rearing difficult at times, but this should not be an indictment against fatherhood as a whole.

Fathers are frequently attacked on the basis of acts performed by a few bad fathers. Good fathers, who I call "Dads," are a silent and mostly invisible group—invisible in the sense that the good they do is in the home and seldom acclaimed by anyone, from TV sitcoms to the local news to *60 Minutes*.

DAD TIP:

People—male or female—who allow their actions and relationships to be informed by the actions of TV characters, sports heroes, or entertainment figures may be asking for trouble. Each parent needs to think for him or herself. Your values should be your values, not those of a folk hero or a fictional character.

YOUR KIDS NEED BOTH PARENTS

Even if a man and a woman have similar values to teach their offspring, they likely have different strengths in relating to their children. Children need the diversity of ideas presented by both a mother and a father. They need a masculine and a feminine approach, a yin and a yang, different approaches and viewpoints. Differing views often complement each other.

As an example, we can assume for a moment that females and mothers are generally more socially aware and concerned for those in society who may need help. Women often are led by their hearts. Males and fathers may tend to advocate self-responsibility and want those who appear helpless to become strong. Men often are led by their beliefs. For example, a mother may be more likely to subsidize an adult son living at home, while a father may be more likely to kick him out to motivate him to find a job.

Whether this is true in your family or not, it does point out the need for different viewpoints our children should be exposed to. They need a diversity of thought and opinions to ponder and discuss. A lesson or technique that works for one child may not work for another. Parents need to *share* the responsibility of mentoring.

I heard a relevant discussion at a kitchen table the other day. A mother, stepfather, and three children were discussing a behavior. The oldest child questioned the difference between his parents' discipline of himself (age twelve) and his younger brother (age five).

"We love all of you equally," the parents said. "But what works to teach one child how to behave doesn't necessarily work for all of you. We match our teaching and discipline to what's best for each of you individually. The behaviors we're teaching are equal, even if our way of getting there may not seem equal." This kitchen table discussion also shows us that parents should agree on the important issues of parenthood and not undercut one another's authority.

But these same parents would also agree that it is valuable to have kids ask each parent's opinion as they learn, allowing the children to make their own decisions whenever possible. Allowing children to make their own choices and decisions, with corrections inserted as needed by their parents, is a better approach in preparing them for the future than dictating their every move and making all decisions for them.

A father is different from a mother, and he should be. We are not living in an androgynous society. A boy doesn't need two mothers, and a girl doesn't want two mothers. We need memories of relationships with both genders. We need to learn from both. We need to respect both.

Mothers and fathers discipline differently, protect differently, and think differently; their expectations of their children are often different. A Mom can appreciate what the Dad can offer in raising their children, even if she would not do it the same way. And Dads appreciate the things Moms do, which are often those tasks that fathers feel less capable of handling.

The valuable lessons a child must learn and prepare for in life require a lot of time and attention, much more time than a father or a mother alone could provide. If the mother most often takes care of the daily needs of her children, then the father can supplement and share in this daily care as both parents play a significant role in preparing their children for the future.

When he is loving and responsible, the natural father is *the* best partner for the mother, in raising their children.

CULTURE AND PARENTAL FOCUS

The social implications of poor fathering are quite obvious. But why has poor fathering become a problem in the first place? One reason is that many fathers are not sufficiently educated in the value of giving attention to their children. Women, as a whole, tend to not need as much education in how to be a good mother, many having been surrounded by effective role models throughout their lives. Men, as a whole, tend to need a lot of education in how to be a good father—how to become a real Dad.

While the different natures of man and woman are a factor, culture has also been a major cause of uneven parental focus. Some men are brought up to think that raising children is the mother's responsibility, while the father works to bring home money to support them. Also, mothers get most of the attention just before, during, and after birth.

"We are often so anxious to affirm a close and uninterrupted attachment between baby and mother that in the service of

early 'mother-infant bonding' we unwittingly disrupt the baby's early connection to the father."

—Kyle D. Pruett,
"How Men and Children Affect Each Other's Development"

Though responsibility is the hallmark of good parenting, raising a child is not looked upon as a "manly" endeavor in some lower socio-economic circles. And across all strata of society, to self-indulgent men, having a baby is all about themselves. If they get a woman pregnant, they think it's the woman's "fault" for being too available or not insisting on protection. These unsophisticated men can't be bothered with "their [i.e., the woman's] mistake," nor can they be held down by a child they do not want. Selfishness, shame, laziness, ignorance of their roles, indifference, fear, and lack of encouragement are all reasons why some men (often boys) are not responsible fathers.

In Robert Coles's *The Moral Intelligence of Children*, Delia, a young single mother of a six-month-old girl, presents a chilling account of a world where young men do not seek to be fathers but predators, looking to outperform their buddies in the game of being "bad."

Delia says of these men, "They're copying the men they saw, growing up—trying to be big, big, big shots. Knock up the girls, one after the other! Play nice with them, give to them, until they give in, then walk away, and when you hear they're carrying, carve another one on your big belt: yo, look at me, you guys, I'm taller than anyone, 'the fastest guy around,' they brag to each other, in-out, in-out—that's what you hear."

A FATHERLESS FAMILY

My wife, Kathy, is a parent educator who specializes in teaching teen parents how to best raise and prepare their children for school. Here's a description of a situation in a mini-culture called "the fatherless family" in which one of my wife's former teen parents, now thirty years old, finds herself:

This woman—I'll call her Rose—has eight children whom she bore with seven different fathers (she has one set of twins). With this many children, she does not work and is on welfare. Rose's mother and grandmother help with the children, but no men are involved. Rose herself never had a father present. Now her eight beautiful children are being raised without their fathers.

Rose is not alarmed because she has no reference of having a father herself. Only the father of the eighth child is involved with any of the children. My wife doesn't expect him be involved for long. When I met Rose, this father was serving a jail sentence for selling drugs. Rose doesn't think of her children's fathers as fathers. She thinks of them as her past boyfriends.

According to Kathy, Rose is a good mother and a sweet girl, but she is not thinking about the impact of raising her children without their fathers, never having had one involved in her own life. If I had to guess, based on experience and statistics, some of her daughters will have children without being married, and her sons will not know what it means to be a father to a child. Variations of Rose's situation occur much more frequently than most of us are aware. Children often live their lives the only way they know how, mimicking the situation in which they were raised. (Note: Since I first wrote this, one of Rose's daughters is now pregnant but not in a serious relationship.)

THE CONSEQUENCES OF RAISING CHILDREN WITHOUT CARING FATHERS

The behavior, confidence, achievements, attitudes, and futures of children are tremendously influenced by fathers. In my own circumstance, I had a father who was occasionally present but not involved. My behavior was shaped by my own shyness and timidity, my confidence was nil, my achievements came about mostly from fear of failure, and my attitude was one of "let me get through this."

Would I have had these traits with a caring father present to mentor me? Maybe, but having a caring father would most likely have helped my attitude, minimized my timidity, helped me to achieve more than I did, and thereby would have helped build my confidence. I had it in me to succeed all along, and with a little encouragement, I would have done so sooner and with budding self-assurance.

Instead, I felt like a duck in a shooting gallery—out there in the world and vulnerable, seemingly without choices and hoping I would get through unscathed. The often dire challenges of a fatherless life are preventable only by the presence of good fathers. As fathers, we can minimize the natural weaknesses and negative tendencies of our children by getting involved right from the beginning.

DAD TIP:

The most manly characteristic is to accept the responsibility of fathering a child. Becoming involved is the greatest gift a father can give. *Nowhere should it be considered acceptable for a man to leave his children and their mother behind. To not accept responsibility is to leave your children at risk.*

A CONTINUING CHALLENGE

Families have always had problems. Father absence, whether physical or emotional, has been at the forefront of the reasons why.

In the last two hundred years, this paternal absence could be laid at the feet of shorter life spans of the past, wretched working conditions of the Industrial Age, or the "want it now," work-work-work needs of ego-driven families of today. But whatever the generational reason, the lack of a fatherly figure in the home has significantly contributed to family turmoil.

Challenges continue to appear as society changes. Offspring used to depend on their parents and grandparents to learn a skill, such as sewing a dress or building a barn. Now parents rely on their offspring to teach them how to use a smartphone or set up a wireless network. This fact tends to cloud who is dependent on whom and can take a little of the hierarchal structure away from the parents.

In just the last few decades, we have seen increased life spans, easier divorces, wider use of birth control, changing moral attitudes, a rise in two-income families, the acceptance of daycare, and a reliance on television, the Internet, video games, and cable news for education and entertainment. One could argue each of these examples to be either positive or negative with regard to parenting. Generally, these arguments hinge on how society handles the change, not the change itself. For example, technology is not inherently bad, but using it as a babysitter, or allowing it to become an obsession for you or your children, can be very troublesome.

Fathers of today have a large variety of challenges that men of days past did not have, but we also have more choices. Certainly, we have an advantage over colonial fathers who often died before their children were grown. And we do not usually have to work fourteen-hour days in the fields just to feed our families. The key issue, no matter the surrounding circumstances, is based on relationships. Fathers who can focus on and nurture relationships can overcome the issues of the day. They're the ones who make the leap from being a father to a real Dad.

DAD TIP:

Men who accept their roles as fathers can become Dads. These men focus on and nurture relationships with their children. No matter what the cultural issues are, involved Dads can help a family overcome adversity.

LOVE OR MONEY?

It is a social rarity in America to excuse an absent father from meeting his financial responsibilities. What is sadly accepted is excusing him from his fatherly responsibilities. As stated by Blankenhorn in *Fatherless America*: "In our cultural model of the Deadbeat Dad, the core issue is money absence, not father absence." Discussion of the absence of a father always seems to center on the need for income—child support. While income is important, the lack of a male role model and the lack of a real, involved Dad—truly supporting the child—is the real problem. Those of us who are worried about a fatherless America (and I wish there were more of us) realize that the best way to get men to support their children is to help these men become better fathers. It is easier to become a deadbeat dad when:

- you think of sex but not the consequences
- you haven't had the mentoring many young men need to be a nurturing father
- you are confused and afraid
- the mother doesn't want you around
- you have little or no money
- you feel you have no control over the child or the money you send
- you are looked down upon—described as a terrible partner or parent—when the facts of the matter may prove differently

While the hurdles can be daunting, you can overcome them if you want to. But before that happens, you have total control over becoming a father, or becoming a father again. If you have any doubts or questions about ever being a father or even having more children, read the next chapter, "To Be or Not to Be." Otherwise, you can skip it and move on to understanding the negative social impacts that can arise with fatherless children, which you can help minimize by being a good Dad.

YOUR ROAD MAP: CHAPTER 2

Start: Determine right now that you will not allow "father absence" to define you. Ever.

Major Highway: You and your children's mother determine the values with which they are raised. Your challenge is to work together, through thick and thin. You will be bombarded by opinions and "role models" in the world of media and entertainment. Keep to your own road. Don't be influenced by these uninspirational models, whether fictional or real.

On the Open Road: Imagine how your life would have been different if you had a) a father's presence, b) a Dad's presence, or c) no positive male role model. Now imagine your child and his or her need for your involvement. What kind of a father are you choosing to be?

Second Stop: Think about where you are on your road to Dadhood. What is working well? What is lacking? Look at your role from the perspective of your children. Look at your role from the perspective of your children's mother. What do you want to change? What can you do to reach a higher level on the Pyramid of Dadhood that we discussed earlier or to improve your actions on the level you're currently on?

CHAPTER 3

TO BE
OR NOT TO BE

"Some men just aren't cut out for paternity. Better they should realize it before and not after they become respon-sible for a son."

—Lois McMaster Bujold, *Ethan of Athos*

INVOLVEMENT AND LOVE

A column heading caught my eye as I was paging through my daily paper just before writing today. It read, "Husband is willing to father baby but wouldn't interact with it." It seems this man's wife wanted a baby but he, most definitely, did not. However, he loved his wife and did not want to "grow apart" from her, and although he disliked children, he agreed he would father a child for his wife. But, he stated, "[I will] probably avoid ours as much as possible." This guy most likely thinks he is being gener-ous to his wife. But I'm not sure I've heard of a more self-centered person in my life.

I like what the syndicated columnist Carolyn Hax had to say in the last paragraph of her scathing response: "Not everyone who has children loves to be around children. But it would be unconscionable to have one when you don't feel a profound sense of responsibility to be there, and to show steady, devoted, and fierce love and support."

She's absolutely right. But this man is not alone in his abhorrence of fatherhood.

FATHERHOOD IS NOT FOR EVERY MAN

There are many reasons why we don't do things we should. Some of those reasons include: We don't want to. We don't think we want to. We're afraid to fail. We don't think about it. We don't have time. We don't make time. We are selfish. We are weak. We are stupid. We are uneducated and confused.

Let's address these reasons as they apply to not wanting to be a father.

Reason	Solution
I don't want to.	Then you must take steps to *not* become one.
I don't think I want to.	Then don't become one until you *know* for sure that you want to.
I'm afraid to fail.	Then don't fail to take proper precautions and preparations.
I don't think about it.	Think about it very seriously.
I don't have time.	Then you must *take* time for proper precautions.
I don't make time.	Then you must *make* time for proper precautions.
I am selfish.	Then don't be so selfish that you don't take proper precautions.
I am weak.	Then be strong enough to admit it.
I am stupid.	Then be smart enough to take proper precautions.
I am uneducated and confused.	Then learn about the responsibilities of a father before you become one.

To those of you who don't want to be a father, you have now received the most important message that applies to you.

> **DAD TIP:**
> *There is nothing wrong with* not *wanting to be a father.* But if you don't want to be a father, you must take precautions to not become one. *Don't leave that responsibility to anyone else.*

TO BE OR NOT TO BE . . .

There is nothing wrong with a man who decides he doesn't want to be a father. I applaud those men who realize this and take all steps necessary to *not* become one. To those noble men, I say this: You can now close this book and pass it on to a brother, friend, or any man you know who *is* interested in being a father or who would like to be a better father. But if you are *already* a father, you must think now of someone other than yourself. To those who choose to be fathers or choose actions that cause them to be fathers, you would be wise to understand the critical role you play in another human life.

> **DAD TIP:**
> *Let's look at this chapter's introductory quotation again, with a few changes:* "Some men just aren't cut out for paternity. Better they should realize it before and not after they become responsible for a son or daughter."

Being a loving, involved father is a rewarding role in a far different sense than you will experience as a successful businessman, craftsman, politician, or sports figure. Fatherly rewards come through minuscule acts that don't get much attention. They come from acts that are totally unselfish, yet uniquely satisfying.

MAYBE LATER

You may want to become a father, but this is not the time, or your current priorities, lifestyle, educational opportunities, social situation, ability to provide a safe home environment, or other circumstances make it unwise to move forward. Then wait until you feel comfortable in your ability to meet new and challenging responsibilities. This *attitude* shows an *aptitude* to be a wonderful and successful Dad.

YOUR ROAD MAP: CHAPTER 3

Start: Decide whether or not you want to father a child.

Major Highway: Either take responsibility to have a child and become involved in his or her life, or take the responsibility and precautions to prevent conceiving a baby.

On the Open Road: Imagine your life as a dad. Think how your action of fathering a child will affect the life of the child's mother, the child, and yourself. Carefully consider the choice you make.

Third Stop: Think about what is required. As a man, you can have sex. As a father, you have conceived a child. As a Dad, you are part of your child's life and lead him or her with love, nurturing, comfort, and stability. What is your choice? Are you ready to take on the joys, and the challenges, of being an involved father—a Dad?

CHAPTER 4

THE SOCIAL IMPLICATIONS OF AN ABSENT FATHER

"To tolerate the trend of fatherlessness is to accept the inevitability of continued societal recession."

—David Blankenhorn, *Fatherless America*

FATHERS: THE FIRST LINE OF DEFENSE FOR A HEALTHY SOCIETY

In any society you will find:

- Child abuse
- Education issues

- Poverty
- Crime
- Emotional and behavioral problems
- Inappropriate sexual activity involving minors

But in a society where few fathers are engaged with their children, these issues explode.

In his book *Fatherless America*, Blankenhorn theorizes that devalued fatherhood has led to a higher incidence of crime, domestic violence, child sexual abuse, and child poverty. Beyond theory, I think the forthcoming statistics will make that quite clear.

It's undeniable that the preponderance of families with strong parents have children with far fewer "issues." Expand that to a nation of good mothers and fathers, and I guarantee that nation will be one of the strongest nations in the world, with much less dependence on social programs, military might, natural resources, or geographic location, because an entire society built on solid parenting would be virtually unshakable and morally strong.

As stated by Linda Eyre in her co-authored book, *The Turning*:

> Nothing is more responsible for the pain and suffering in the world than the breakdown of families; nothing can heal and renew the world like the revaluing of families; and there is not nearly enough focus on how dramatically the state of families affects the state of society.

But beyond the big societal picture, children deserve the love of their fathers for their own development and success. It's relatively easy to learn what it takes to become a good Dad, but actually doing it and having successful results is much more difficult. Once you have earned your children's trust, they'll always come back for support and advice, no matter their age.

While young, most children don't consciously know what their parents are up to and may not care. But unconsciously they want to know you will take care of them and love them. You give them this assurance with praise and discipline. They also want to know what to expect from you. They will know what to expect if you are consistent.

And yet, what about those homes where the father is absent?

"For boys, the most socially acute manifestation of paternal disinvestment is juvenile violence. For girls, it is juvenile and out-of-wedlock childbearing. One primary result of growing fatherlessness is more boys with guns. Another is more girls with babies."

—David Blankenhorn, *Fatherless America*

"For the best part of thirty years we have been conducting a vast experiment with the family, and now the results are in: the decline of the two-parent, married-couple family has resulted in poverty, ill-health, educational failure, unhappiness, anti-social behavior, isolation and social exclusion for thousands of women, men and children."

—Rebecca O'Neill, *Experiments in Living: The Fatherless Family*

These quotes put a professional spin on what we already know. But where is the movement to reverse these tragic trends? Instead of fixing the problem, we accept its results.

Our nation's government, like those of other nations, attempts to help those in need. But when it comes to families that must accept government help, we find that most are without fathers. And no matter how hard it tries to provide food, shelter, and medical care for needy families, our government cannot provide the two most important things a child needs from a father: *love and emotional support.*

THE FACTS

- 85 percent of all children who exhibit behavioral disorders come from fatherless homes. (CDC & O'Block)
- 90 percent of all homeless and runaway children are from fatherless homes.

- 71 percent of high school dropouts come from fatherless homes.
- 75 percent of all adolescent patients in chemical abuse centers come from fatherless homes.
- 63 percent of youth who commit suicide are from fatherless homes. (Bureau of the Census & O'Block)
- 70 percent of juveniles in long-term, state-operated institutions come from single-parent homes. (Beck, Kline, and Greenfield)
- 80 percent of rapists motivated by displaced anger come from fatherless homes. (Knight and Prentky)
- Teens without fathers were twice as likely to be involved in early sexual activity and seven times more likely to get pregnant as an adolescent. (Ellis et al.)
- 72 percent of adolescent murderers grew up without fathers. (Cornell, Benedek, and Benedek)

Put another way, children from fatherless homes are (according to Fathers Unite):

- 15.3 times more likely to have behavioral disorders
- 24.3 times more likely to run away
- 6.6 times more likely to drop out of high school
- 4.6 times more likely to commit suicide
- 6.3 times more likely to be in a state-operated institution
- 10.8 times more likely to commit rape
- 6.6 times more likely to become teenage mothers
- 15.3 times more likely to end up in prison while a teenager

Compared to their peers living with both parents, children in single-parent homes had (according to Sedlak and Broadhurst):

- 77 percent greater risk of being physically abused
- 80 percent greater risk of suffering serious injury as a result of abuse
- 120 percent greater risk of being endangered by some type of child abuse

- 87 percent greater risk of being harmed by physical neglect
- 165 percent greater risk of experiencing notable physical neglect
- 74 percent greater risk of suffering from emotional neglect

THE FACTS ARE EASY TO FIND

This data just scratches the surface, and some of it is decades old. It is telling that over the years I worked on this book, I have found few updated studies on the impacts of fatherlessness. Alarmingly, not enough attention is placed on such a serious social dilemma with dire consequences. To learn more and keep up with the latest information, just search the Internet for "fatherless children statistics." You will be amazed at the number of frightening statistics in these references. Here are four helpful websites regarding fatherhood and fatherless children:

- http://fatherhood.about.com/od/fathersrights/a/fatherless_children.htm
- http://www.fathersunite.org
- http://www.fathers.com/
- http://www.fatherhood.org/

As stated by the National Fatherhood Initiative in their book *Father Facts*:

- 24 million children (34 percent) live absent their biological father (Bureau of the Census).
- Nearly 20 million children (27 percent) live in single-parent homes.
- 1.35 million births (33 percent of all births) in 2000 occurred out of wedlock.
- 43 percent of first marriages dissolve within fifteen years, about 60 percent of divorcing couples have children, and approximately one million children each year experience the divorce of their parents.
- More than 3.3 million children live with an unmarried parent and the parent's cohabiting partner. The number of cohabiting couples

with children has nearly doubled since 1990, from 891,000 to 1.7 million today.

- Fathers who live with their children are more likely to have a close, enduring relationship with them than those who do not. The best predictor of father presence is marital status. Compared to children born within marriage, children born to cohabiting parents are three times as likely to experience father absence, and children born to unmarried, non-cohabiting parents are four times as likely to live in a father-absent home.

- About 40 percent of children in father-absent homes have not seen their father at all during the past year, 26 percent of absent fathers live in a different state than their children, and 50 percent of children living without their father have never set foot in their father's home.

- Children who live absent their biological fathers are, on average, at least two to three times more likely to be poor, to use drugs, to experience educational, health, emotional, and behavioral problems, to be victims of child abuse, and to engage in criminal behavior than their peers who live with their married, biological (or adoptive) parents.

- From 1960 to 1995, the proportion of children living in single-parent homes tripled, from 9 percent to 27 percent, and the proportion of children living with married parents declined. However, from 1995 to 2000, the percentage of children living in single-parent homes slightly declined, while the percentage of children living with two married parents remained stable.

- Children with involved, loving fathers are significantly more likely to do well in school, have healthy self-esteem, exhibit empathy and prosocial behavior, and avoid high-risk behaviors such as drug use, truancy, and criminal activity compared to children who have uninvolved fathers.

With this information, can you imagine the significant improvement our society would experience if, by some miracle, *all* fathers, for two or three generations in a row, would be caring, loving, and available?

Beyond the statistics, it is difficult to wrap our minds around the untold numbers of children who are insecure, sad, and depressed as a result of their father-absent homes. As children, they are more anxious, withdrawn, and less popular than their peers. Growing into adults with many challenges to face, they are the quiet victims.

> **DAD TIP:**
> *Use your favorite Internet search engine and enter "fatherless children statistics." You will be astounded at the studies that confirm the need for caring fathers in our society.*

LACK OF FATHERING IS A ROOT CAUSE OF SOCIETAL STRUGGLES

Statistics are certainly not perfect—not all studies agree—and some people will argue about their context, relevance, and accuracy. But the statistics do give a flavor of the problems caused by raising children in father-absent families. Father absence—even being ignored by one's father—causes so many other social ills, which in turn cause more fatherless homes in an often endless cycle.

If you considered just one social problem caused or magnified by a lack of fathering, it would be impossible to ignore how it ripples throughout society. We could choose teen pregnancy, mental health, crime, or any issue, but let's use drug abuse as an example.

As mentioned earlier, drug use by fatherless children is two to three times more prevalent than by those who have present, engaged, and available fathers. And the ripples through society are visible in crime rates, medical costs, crowded prisons, suicides, early deaths caused by drug overdoses, homelessness, and so on—all increased by the drug culture. As our society tries to help these people recover, this affects each of us financially.

> **DAD TIP:**
> *We can stop the cycle of many of society's woes just by making it our goal and our practice to be present, engaged, and available as Dads.*

Sons and daughters who turn to drugs often do so to try to fill a void left in them by absent fathers. Many of these young people also seek love but do so inappropriately, ending up with children conceived not out of love, but out of a need to be loved. As parents, they often try to raise their offspring without a job or money. And too many continue their drug habits, leaving their own children in a state of dire need. These children will characteristically not have both parents involved in their lives. So without intervention, the cycle continues and expands.

> **DAD TIP:**
> *We spend billions of dollars treating a result, drug abuse, while we allow one of its most significant causes, father absence, to be relatively ignored. I can't say it enough: be involved!*

SOCIETY CANNOT REPLACE GOOD PARENTING

When parents lose control of their kids, then society takes over. All society can do is a one-size-fits-all fix that tends to treat all kids the same.

In Cincinnati, a governing Little League council outlawed chatter in baseball like "hey batter, hey batter, *swing!*" Why? Because too many kids went too far in their bravado and chest pounding, encouraged by watching athletes on TV and accepting them as role models (if Dads weren't there to fill that role).

Distractions, such as the opposing team chattering while a kid is at bat, are good life lessons and should be allowed as long as they are not demeaning. When put into perspective by caring parents, these life lessons teach young people that competition, opposition, and struggle will be constants in their lives. They will learn to deal with the "chatter" and move on toward their goals.

Society errs in its practice of awarding all kids in sports and other endeavors, no matter their standing or effort.

> *"We have of late, we Americans, to our detriment, come to love accolades more than genuine achievement."*
> —David McCullough Jr., "You Are Not Special"

In trying not to hurt little Johnny's feelings, we reward mediocrity, and that is not the answer. The answer is rewarding little Johnny for what he does well, not what he does poorly. If the Baseball Hall of Fame rewarded participation and effort instead of results, it would require a much bigger building. Again, this "everyone wins" mentality is a one-size-fits-all reaction to dealing with children's self-image, which does them no favors. We are once again allowing our society to dictate the role of parenting, resolving an issue that parents should handle on a child-by-child basis.

Ah, but to handle things on a child-by-child basis, we need to be engaged as parents. And here we are, back again at the premise of this book: the power of fatherhood—of being a Dad—means being there, listening, caring, and loving. This is how you handle issues on a child-by-child basis: you are present and involved.

A school banned the use of jump ropes in gym class because some kids couldn't jump rope. I can only assume that those who could not jump rope properly were being teased by other children. Society's answer to that predicament was to eliminate the situation. Instead of letting society take control of the situation, parents need to emphasize to their children the importance of being kind and supportive to others, but also being able to ignore teasing and keep trying until they succeed. While some children of good parents may still bully their peers, parents teaching their children to be kind and resilient is much more effective than letting society completely remove potential learning experiences.

> **DAD TIP:**
> *Do you want society to step in to raise your child? Be present, involved, caring, and loving—and this will never be an issue.*

When kids act cruelly, it is usually to fit in with the wrong group or to seek attention at all costs. What if fitting in meant being supportive and empathic and not being demeaning or trying to feel superior? Through teamwork and support, children will be accepted by those groups worth joining.

Many kids who lead are not good leaders, and those who follow sometimes follow the wrong examples. These misinformed and misled kids have not been properly mentored, and it shows. Receiving the guidance and attention of a father is priceless.

A STRONG COUNTRY, WEAK ON CHILDREN'S WELFARE

In February 2007, the United Nations Children's Emergency Fund (UNICEF) released a report that said, among the twenty-one wealthiest nations, the United States was the worst place to raise a child. The United States ranked low on the scale regarding children who eat and talk frequently with their families and had the highest proportion of children living in single-parent families. Single-parenthood was associated with "a greater risk of dropping out of school, of leaving home early, of poorer health, of low skills, and of low pay."

Conversely, the study revealed that children in the Netherlands, Spain, and Greece "were the happiest," and children of the Netherlands, Spain, and Portugal "spent the most time with their families and friends." The evidence in the Netherlands and Spain supports the obvious: children's welfare—their health and happiness—is greatly enhanced by involvement with those they love.

A partial explanation of the report's low ranking of the United States is the competitive nature in the job market, making adults less available to their children. Jonathan Bradshaw, one of the authors of the study, stated, "The findings we got today are a consequence of long-term underinvestment in children. They [the United States and also the United Kingdom, which ranked next to last] don't invest as much in children as continental European countries do." (Farley)

When economic conditions weaken, parental attention suffers as fathers and mothers look for work or struggle to make ends meet. Men's competitive nature to get work trumps their nature to nurture.

THE CYCLE OF DESPAIR

"If you always do what you've always done, you will always get what you've always got."

—Henry Ford

There are two effects of inept fathers. One effect is subtle, often involving those families that look good from the outside but have problems within. The other effect is obvious, where dysfunction is out in the open and the need for government assistance is common.

The subtle effects are emotional or psychological or both, caused when the father is uncaring, overdominant, or not emotionally connected with his children. These effects are sometimes difficult to detect and have consequences that can be overlooked if we are unaware.

When the father doesn't contribute to the support of his family, the obvious effect is economic. When the obvious economic effects are joined with the subtle, psychological effects, we find children and families in the "cycle of despair." Defeated mothers and absent fathers create future defeated mothers and absent fathers.

> **DAD TIP:**
> *Defeated mothers and absent fathers create future defeated mothers and absent fathers.*

An environment of poor parental care, economic challenges, and little character direction begets children with weak self-esteem and poor values. When this happens, it is no surprise that emotional issues, violence, and drugs are more likely to enter a young person's life.

The cycle of despair not only continues but also grows with each generation through increased poverty, more dependence on social programs, and mushrooming emotional issues. People in this cycle see themselves as victims and demand that society fix what is wrong with their lives. I say, of course they are victims—victims of poor parenting, an acquired negative outlook on life, and little understanding of what they can do for themselves to escape the cycle. My undereducated mother and my absent and inept father have alone spawned five father-absent or father-inept families in just two generations. My wife sees the impacts of this ignored truth every day in her job working with teen parents. You have surely seen it yourself.

CONTRIBUTORS TO THE CYCLE OF DESPAIR

Momentum, resistance, fear, and ignorance all contribute to the cycle of despair: the relentless reenactment of conditions that produce children disadvantaged by father absence, by father disengagement, or by father disinterest. Being disadvantaged as a child takes on many forms. If not disadvantaged economically, a child can be disadvantaged socially, psychologically, and emotionally. Being in this cycle is a near-hopeless situation that without some type of intervention, cooperation, or miracle will continue without end. The reasons for the cycle are not difficult to determine, but they are difficult to stop.

Momentum contributes to this cycle because it is so easy to continue with what you know, even if you don't like it. Resistance contributes because it is the most imaginative of our individual characteristics—in other words, we can find so many ways to resist change or to resist those things that will take us to better situations. Fear contributes by being the backbone of resistance (Pressfield). Without fear, there would be no resistance. Ignorance contributes because you cannot make choices when you don't know what your options are or when you lack understanding about the benefits and limitations of those options.

The cycle isn't limited to any particular location, whether rural, urban, or suburban. It can happen anywhere families are at risk.

If you are not a victim of this cycle, then you can prevent it from rearing its ugly head and creating misery for your descendants. If you are a product of this cycle, reading and heeding the advice in this book will help you intervene. You are taking action. You are seeking understanding and wisdom. Good for you—and great for your children. Without your intention to break the cycle of despair, a miracle would certainly be needed to save your children from the same plight.

DAD TIP:

If you are a product of the "cycle of despair," stop right now and give yourself a pat on the back. Just by seeking advice through reading and practicing the tips in this book, you are breaking the cycle of despair.

Eradicate the *ignorance* that prevents better choices. By reading this book, heeding its advice, and recommending it to others, you are doing that now. Removing ignorance brings enlightenment, which will help break the *momentum* of questionable life choices. Enlightenment lessens *fear* by helping you see that you are not alone and that there are tools and resources to help you. Lessening fear will weaken the *resistance* to change and the excuses you have used so cleverly to avoid or shirk your fatherly duties.

WE LEARN FROM OUR ENVIRONMENT—AND THE PEOPLE IN IT

A meme is a cultural behavior or style transmitted by repetition in a manner analogous to the biological transmission of genes. Put simply, "monkey see, monkey do." Infants will learn from abusive adults or unloving adults just as naturally as they will learn from well-meaning, nurturing, and loving adults.

Nature has given us fingers with opposable thumbs, but our genes do not help us decide what to use those fingers for and what behaviors to emulate. Genetic behavior will prompt teens to procreate voluntarily, but the social mores they have learned from their parents may likely determine if they will wait for the right time and person. Similarly, teens need the guidance of adults to combat what their nature and peers tell them to do. Parents must do for their offspring what their offspring's genetic makeup cannot.

If children and teenagers come from an environment that hasn't taught those social mores, nor the value of self-esteem and the lessons of a successful life, then the odds of getting out of their environmental rut are stacked against them. We are shaped by both our genes and our memes.

IT IS IN THE HOME . . .

- where children should learn kindness, goodness, values, discipline, and manners.
- where children should find understanding, care, and comfort.
- where successful lives should begin, with open minds, encouragement, and love.
- where compassion should exist, where the safety nets of our children's failures are made of rubber bands, ready to sling them back into the world—stronger, wiser, and with new momentum.

If we were to find these characteristics in all homes, what kind of world would we have? Certainly most homes have some of these characteristics, a lucky few have most, and some have none. I don't have to spout statistics, although they are readily available, to convince you that in those homes where fathers are present and involved, the chances for success and happiness are much greater.

In *Man Enough*, Frank Pittman explains:

> Being a father, to our own children or to someone else's, or being something like a father—an uncle, a mentor, a coach, a teacher, a therapist—is the real way to become a man. We gain our masculinity not by waving it from flagpoles or measuring and testing it before cheering crowds but by teaching it to boys and girls, and to men and women who haven't known a man up close and don't know what men and masculinity are all about. *If men would raise children, it would not only save the world in a generation or two, it would save their lives.*

THE INFLUENCE OF RELATIONSHIPS

When I think of what was good and bad in my childhood, it always comes back to relationships. Those relationships could be with friends, teachers, or siblings, or with a stranger whose kind words during a brief encounter had a lasting impact. When I was nine years old, a stranger watched me learn to ice skate on a Saturday afternoon and told me what a good job I did. That kind and encouraging statement has stayed with me all these years.

Certainly teachers and others can have a huge influence on our lives, but without a doubt the parent-child relationship is the most important of all, especially for the child. Nothing will impact you more—not marriage, not even your own children—compared to your childhood relationship with your parents.

Not to belittle its huge importance in our lives, but even marriage pales in comparison to our upbringing. None of your core values will change much with marriage. (Of course your life will change. Having children will change your life forever, but in ways different from establishing your core values or personality.) All of us were tremendously influenced by our parents, and our most lasting influence will be *as* a parent.

DAD TIP:

If you came from a home with an absent father, you likely still had positive male influences in your life—people who helped you form your core values. As a father, your most lasting influence will be as a parent. What type of man do you choose to be? A father, or a Dad?

Nurturing parents consciously create an environment that lets children shape themselves within proper limitations and guidelines. We as parents provide the mold that represents those limitations and guidelines.

A BETTER SOCIETY, ONE CHILD AT A TIME

On November 5, 2011, an article appeared in the *Augusta Chronicle* entitled "Poor Parenting Leads Youth to Violent Crime." The article, written by Meg Mirshak, reported on violent acts perpetrated by very young children, tying it to poor parenting. What caught my attention, however, was a comment by a user called literallyamerican.

> I visited a prison not long ago to see the guy who killed my sister. I was looking to understand what happened and why he would do something like that. When I sat there looking around at everyone in the room where people visit, I was shocked to see so many young men in there. It became aware to me, looking at their faces, that for the first time in their lives, they were experiencing what *real* boundaries are. I believe in punishment and fully realize that you have to pay for what you do, but in some ways it was sad because they had to come to prison to get that type of "parenting" that should have been done at home. I saw the same thing in the person I went to confront—he looked completely shell shocked.

Juvenile court judges, therapists, police, and social workers will all tell you that most young people who get into trouble do not have a father at home, and if they do, he is not involved in fathering his children. It is not my intention to place blame or a guilt trip on anyone. The social implications of ineffective fathers are indeed severe, but my real intention is to make it absolutely clear how much of a hero each man would be to his family, that small nugget of society, by just doing what he is supposed to do as a father: to simply be there and care. We men don't understand the good we do, the problems we prevent, and the happiness we bring, unless we look at what happens when we don't perform our role as fathers.

WE'RE OBLIGATED TO PAY ATTENTION

> *"I think it's such a lucky accident, having been born, that we're almost obliged to pay attention."*
> —Mark Strand, quoted in Mihaly Csikszentmihalyi, *Creativity*

The miracle and privilege of life is the gift most often taken for granted by us human beings. You are not just the result of the gleam in your father's eye; you are the culmination of all the events occurring since infinity. It could have been that one citizen of an ancient culture was drawn to the left fork in the road by a shade tree grown from a seed, carried by an animal that survived a drought while its natural predator did not. This citizen continued down this chosen path and impacted a history that made your presence today possible. If not for that dry, hot summer, maybe thousands of years ago, our citizen of the ancient past may well have taken a different path and led a different life; you, with your looks, personality, and potential, would not be here.

Now you, too, will have an impact on a future that extends beyond your own lineage. There is not the slightest doubt of the significant influence you will have on your children, their children, and on and on. Our DNA, and the culture we teach and exhibit, will mold our children. In this vast perspective, we should embrace our tremendous responsibilities as men and as parents.

Blankenhorn states in *Fatherless America*: "In all societies, child well-being and societal success hinge largely upon a high level of paternal investment: the willingness of adult males to devote energy and resources to the care of their offspring."

YOUR ROAD MAP: CHAPTER 4

Start: Admit the social impact of father absence.

Major Highway: Realize your impact, as a man, on your children's lives. If you are a father, consider carefully the path you have chosen. Are you a Dad—involved, available, teaching? Or are you a father—at home, but not involved? Or are you an absent father? It is never too late to change your path to a more positive role.

On the Open Road: Remember your life as a child. What was your relationship with your father like? How has this shaped the way you father your children? What have you chosen to repeat? What have you chosen to overcome?

Fourth Stop: Think about the way the world—not just American society, but the whole world—would improve if father absence were eradicated for just two generations. What can you do to ensure that father absence is partially erased in your generation? What personal path will you choose?

THE
CHALLENGES OF
FATHERHOOD

CHAPTER 5

THE CHALLENGES OF BEING A KID

"If you think being an adult is tough, just try being a kid!"
—Any kid

Sometimes we think our children have it easy. We feed, clothe, and shelter them, and all they have to do is play, do a couple of chores, and go to school. What we may forget is the apprehension, anxiety, fear, shaky confidence, and need for acceptance that all kids have. There are bullies to deal with, the judgment of adults, fear of the dark, and many other obstacles children face as they grow up. And to make it worse, they don't have a lot of experience in dealing with this stuff. As a father, it is your job to guide and coach your children through their challenges.

CHALLENGE OF CHILDREN'S FEAR

"Many of our fears are tissue-paper-thin, and a single coura-geous step would carry us clear through them."

—Brendan Francis Behan

No one likes to be afraid. As a father, you especially don't want your children to be afraid. But some fears are helpful because they keep us and our children safe.

For adults, fear may be described as a healthy respect. Respect for the power of the ocean, respect for authority, respect for the dangers of traffic, and so on. These are healthy attitudes to keep us alert and aware of danger. For children, it's natural to sometimes be afraid, and these rational fears help protect them. True, some kids appear to have no fear, but it's often a lack of respect for situations that can put them in danger or get them into trouble.

As adults, we can often acknowledge that many of our fears are irrational and inhibiting. Irrational fears are roadblocks to our progress as individuals and interfere with the enjoyment of our lives. They often begin in childhood. Fear keeps some of our children from making friends. Fear prevents others from exploring new adventures. Thunder can make children want to crawl under the bed, but then they are afraid of what's under the bed. And speaking in front of people can paralyze anyone. The fears our children don't understand are the ones they try to avoid. When avoidance is allowed to continue, fear remains. As the years go by, resistance to facing these fears grows greater, and this resistance makes the fears more difficult to overcome because we never prove them false.

When I was in eighth grade, I was sick once and missed three or four days of school. When it was time to go back, I was terrified. In my mind, I would be behind in work and completely lost. I assumed my classmates would look at me and wonder, "What's his problem?" I anticipated the teacher would give me looks of disgust for not being there.

Feigning more sickness, I fought my mom about going back to school. She let me get away with it until I had missed almost two weeks. Finally, I went back when I agreed with my mom to visit the principal, who I assumed would somehow make it easier for me. He did—by sending me straight to my classroom. When I got back into class, everything was just fine. My worries were unfounded.

I went home that night delirious with relief that it was all over. I had been paralyzed by fear. As many kids do, I thought the universe noticed me more than it did. A concerned and present father perhaps would have kicked me out of the house and sent me back to school. That's what I needed. This experience proved to me that fear is the backbone of resistance. Resistance fed by fear can keep you from experiences that bring joy and variety into your life. Freedom from irrational fear is a true blessing.

> **DAD TIP:**
> *We resist change with all our might when we are afraid. As Dads, we help our children meet their fears head on. We stand beside them as they conquer their demons. We can't do it for them, but we can be there with them.*

Fear can also be a beacon, shining the way to what you want to achieve. In *The War of Art*, Steven Pressfield states, "Fear is good. Like self-doubt, fear is an indicator. Fear tells us what we have to do." He goes on to explain that the more we fear and resist something, the more important that "something" is to us. The sooner we meet the challenge of that fear, the sooner we will grow as a person. We need to pass this knowledge to ourselves first, learn its value, believe in it, and then pass it on to our children.

FACING FEAR: THE SUREST WAY TO DEFEAT IT

Facing your fears will open doors that were previously nailed closed. As a young boy and well into my adult years, I didn't realize that facing my fears would work so well to defeat them. I realize now that a more present father could have helped me overcome my fears.

Since I never learned to charge ahead despite my fears, my method of handling fear turned to avoidance and procrastination. The fear was never defeated; it just hovered over and around me at all times. I know this had a profound impact on my early life. All the challenges I did not accept and all the opportunities that had frightened me away were lost. Had I only taken on some of those challenges and opportunities, I would have been happier sooner, set and achieved even more goals, and become a better father myself.

When I was about eight years old, I didn't know how to swim. My mother had a friend who had a pool with a deep end, way deeper than I was tall. This friend knew I was afraid to go past the rope that divided the deep water from the shallow water, and he also knew that if I lost a little of the fear of being in water over my head, he could teach me to swim. His first step was to talk me into slowly getting into the pool at the deep end and holding on to the side. He then said, "I want you to drop down to the bottom, and when you get there, just push up with your feet and grab back onto the side. Just know I'll be right here so you don't have to worry about anything." I drifted to the bottom, just as he said, and when my feet felt the rough floor of the pool, I bent my knees a bit, pushed up, and popped out of the water. I was so proud of myself.

With this success, I was feeling adventurous and open to the next step. My mom's friend had me stand by the deep end of the pool and told me to dive in, head first, toward the shallow end. He told me if I just kicked with my feet and pulled with my arms, I would glide to the shallow end easily. My newfound confidence allowed me to take the plunge. Again, he was right, and I easily glided to the shallow end. I cannot explain the conquering feeling I experienced. I was soon swimming on my own and had rid myself of a huge fear in my life. Eureka!

That lesson was not just how to lose my fear of the water, but *how to face my fears in order to conquer them*. With a little help from a mentor, I was able to face my fear of deep water, and by facing it, the fear vanished.

When you don't know how to swim, the fear of deep water is natural and protecting. My fear of the water was protecting me until I learned to swim. However, my fear of "facing my fear" was restricting my personal growth. If facing your fear works for natural fear, it will certainly work for unnatural, uncommon, or unreasonable fears. Unfortunately, that bigger lesson escaped me when I was eight, and as it turned out, I had unreasonable fears well into my adulthood. I wish I had had a mentor to help me learn this sooner. A father or mentor can do the little things that help you grow into a balanced, healthy person.

> ### DAD TIP:
> Never *belittle anyone's fears, especially those of your children. We all have our own experiences, neuroses, weaknesses, and strengths. You are not helping others when you judge their fears as baseless or of no consequence. A few encouraging words from a Dad will help a child face fear and may prevent years of self-generated grief.*

HELPING CHILDREN FACE FEAR ON THEIR OWN

My mother's pool friend helped me face my fear directly. A second method to help your children with their fears is to place them in an environment where they must face the feared situation on their own, with no direct influence or interference from you, the father (or mother). Real confidence is gained when your children tackle their demons on their own. An independent act of facing fear will fuel an independent attitude and confidence.

For example, if your children are uncomfortable with social situations, get them involved in Boy Scouts, Girl Scouts, a sports team, or something similar. And challenging your children in this way doesn't just apply to overcoming fears—if they are always in the house and not playing outside, then give them things they have to do outside, or don't allow them to watch TV or play video games at certain times of the day.

Ultimately, helping children overcome fear on their own still requires you to play a part. Your role is to notice your children's struggle and place them in a situation that will allow them to gain confidence from handling the fear. When positive steps take place, praise your child not just for the success, but also for the courage it took to move forward.

CAUTION BEFRIENDS THE ADVENTUROUS AND BETRAYS THE MEEK

The principle taught in this section heading is again a matter of balance. Whereas a bold son or daughter may need to be reeled in a bit, a mild-mannered child may need a push toward adventure. We as parents, and especially fathers, provide the counterbalance to what we perceive is a child's tendency toward adventurous behavior or meekness. It is not unusual to have one child who has to be talked into things and another who needs to be talked *out* of things. Spare judgment on either and *be careful not to compare.*

I was hesitant about handling worms when I was a little kid. My younger brother, Steve, however, didn't think twice about hooking a worm. I was a little ashamed of that. If my father had known this, I would have liked him to help me get over this fear. It first had to be noticed by a caring person. Then that person could have shown me in a gentle way how to lose the fear. Instead I held that shame, as small as it was, inside me for quite some time. Now I fear no worm.

THE CHALLENGE OF PEER PRESSURE

How we *want* people to see us versus how we *think* people see us can cause a lot of anxiety. One of the burdens of my life was lifted when I finally accepted how I was and how people viewed me. Accepting both, the facts and the perceptions, allows you to not be worried about others' opinions of you.

My good fortune in learning this attitude came a bit later than I would have liked, but your child can learn it sooner with your help. Although I worried constantly about what people thought of me, I did not succumb to peer pressure. That strength helped keep me from smoking, stealing, pulling destructive pranks, or taking drugs. I can't explain how I came about this characteristic, but I know others, just as mysteriously, fall deeply into the traps of peer pressure. I consider myself fortunate in this respect. Of course, I was not totally free of peer pressure. No one really is.

All young people probably suffer the pangs of peer pressure to varying degrees. They often worry more about what their peers think than they do about the opinions of their parents, teachers, or other adults. Being supremely image-conscious, many young people's lives are tremendously impacted by how they are treated or seen by peers. Here's where being aware of your child's tendencies and being observant can clue you in on when to intercede or give guidance. It's good to remind your kids that no one can know them as well as they know themselves.

DAD TIP:

If you find your child is treated a certain negative way by his or her peers, it could be useful information with which to evaluate your child or the situation. You may be able to resolve the issue after quietly researching or consulting with experts. In the meantime, teach your child these words: "You have control over your actions—not anyone else."

How could we possibly know the motivations of people who degrade or are cruel to others? Children, even friends, can be envious, jealous, self-absorbed, busy, angry, or lacking in confidence of their own. It could be that your child just misinterprets something said or done to him or her. Teach your children this: "You must not allow yourself to be too sensitive to what others say or to think too much. All you need to know is that *you* have control over your actions—not anyone else."

Here is one of those little truths we all know, but too few practice. To change anything about yourself, you must "fake it 'til you make it," which is a way to remind yourself constantly of the things you know are true, but don't yet believe to be in your control.

THE CHALLENGE OF CONFIDENCE

Self-confidence can be nurtured by introducing your child to challenging experiences, such as hiking the Grand Canyon, cleaning a fish, or joining a drama club. Kids become self-confident when they get over the fear of the unknown, when they overcome an inhibition, and when they accept that they don't have to be good at everything, because no one has ever been good at everything.

The challenge must not exceed their capacity, or their confidence could diminish. Nor should you mislead them into falsely thinking they've achieved a significant success when it was too easily attained. Success does build confidence, but success built on sand will not contribute to your child's confidence in the long run. Confidence gained by easy victories can be shattered by reality.

> **DAD TIP:**
> *A Dad can teach his child self-confidence with these words: "You don't have to be good at everything. No one is good at everything!"*

It may not be wise to convince your children that they are great artists or athletes if they will be judged more honestly in school or by friends. A more realistic view will not set them up for a fall, a fall from which recovery could be difficult. But, of course, praise any real talent and encourage any talent that shows promise.

Confidence is not just expecting success, but also not fearing failure.

A confident person looks at failure as a wall in a maze: they just turn in another direction and keep going until they find their reward. When your children don't make attempts, it is often because they don't want to try and then fail, not because they can't do it. Successes met after a few failures are much more satisfying and are great lessons in perseverance.

You can also teach your children that trying and failing is only a limited failure that could eventually lead to success with further attempts, whereas failure to try at all is total failure. Our children will learn they can survive these limited failures and will have the confidence to try new things. Newfound confidence is like grease, easing the friction of a new situation. Guarantees are not necessary for the confident child.

How do you find the right experiences for your kids, the kind that will give them confidence? Just listen to them and watch them. By this I don't mean spying on them or continually following them around. Just pay attention to their tendencies when challenged and faced with obstacles, and take action when necessary. What do you notice they shy away from? What events, people, things, and experiences do they tend to avoid? If you notice something, ask them about it. They may deny avoiding whatever you have noticed, or they may admit to a fear or anxiety about a situation. Don't make a big deal about it; just give an encouraging word.

MEETING CHALLENGES AND BUILDING CONFIDENCE

> *"God gives every bird its food, but he doesn't throw it into its nest."*
>
> —J. G. Holland

When lions are cubs, the mother lioness nourishes them. Later on, they must learn how to hunt or they will starve. Animals know there is a time to care for their young and a time to teach them to be on their own.

We must do the same, but instead of teaching our offspring how to find food, we humans need to teach a different kind of survival. We teach them how to meet challenges and obstacles on their own and to avoid the tricks of the mind—those mind games that can steal their confidence, faith, independence, and dreams. To do that for our children takes a lot of observing, hand wringing, strength, coaching, and love. But that is what a nurturing father does. That's what makes you a Dad.

My kids, like most, wanted me (or their mom) to solve their problems for them. We refused to do so if we thought they could handle it on their own. If my son broke a neighbor's window, he would have to break the news to the neighbor. If one of my daughters lost a schoolbook, she would have to find a way to make it right. They sometimes hated that we would make them face the responsibility of a situation they created. But after they did, it became an uplifting experience and a lesson in confidence. They felt good about meeting a challenge and recognizing they had survived.

INTEND IS A STRONGER WORD THAN *CAN*

Because feeling confident was an infrequent experience during my childhood and early adulthood, some of my insecurities were probably picked up by my son. It's still difficult to convince him of his abilities and potential; however, he's a man now and continues to grow and succeed.

When I ask myself why he succeeds, it comes down to intent. My son, Mike, didn't think he could graduate from college, but he did. He didn't think he would survive Army basic training, but he did. He didn't think he would become a warrant officer, but he did. He didn't think he could become an Army helicopter pilot, but he did. What he does have, if not an abundance of confidence, is intent. He *intended* to reach these goals despite his fear of failure. His intent has been a key factor in his continued success.

Knowing you *can* makes your *intentions* that much easier, without all the gut-wrenching anxiety. However, many people *can*, or think they can, but never *do*. People with a can-do attitude have their wheels greased, but they have no engine if they have no intent. If we Dads and our children have both the engine (intention) and the grease (confidence), we have what we need to move forward. Not only can we get somewhere, but we can get there with little friction.

THE CHALLENGE OF ATTITUDE

Attitudes are highly important and can have a major impact on your child's emotional and mental growth. Being confident, enthusiastic, optimistic, and courageous are all good attitudes. Attitude alone can make your child a winner or a loser. When you think your children are old enough to understand, teach them to never be a victim or feel sorry for themselves.

Many people love the feeling of being a victim. I should know; I was pretty good at it. The victim attitude is the "feel good" replacement when things aren't going your way. In a strange way, it feels comforting and satisfying, like everyone will feel bad for you, or you are allowed to feel bad for yourself. You expect sympathy and feel deserving of it. *When you are a victim, you are in a position of weakness. It will never get you anywhere.* You can help your children develop good attitudes by knowing when, and when not, to sympathize with them.

It would be appropriate to sympathize with your child when a pet is lost. Sympathy with natural feelings and expressions is supportive. But when the child goes beyond what is natural, say, when your child is throwing a tantrum because he or she cannot have a toy at the toy store, all sympathy must stop. If you sympathize with a child when they don't get their way, you are supporting their pouting and reinforcing a harmful attitude about life.

As a parent, you help your kids *develop* good attitudes by *supporting* good attitudes. A good attitude is a key ingredient in achieving goals, having confidence, and being persistent, and is important in being likable.

THE CHALLENGE OF MANNERS

Good manners will beget acceptance. The basic principles of parenting include teaching your children to like themselves and be likable. I can't imagine not liking any kid with good manners and a positive attitude. Age, looks, intelligence—everything else pales to good manners and positivity when it comes to likability.

There are teens in my neighborhood so likable, I find any excuse to engage with them. There are others who are cold, never say hello, and are always looking down to the ground. When I have tried to be friendly, they mostly shrug. I've known them all since they were born. Mind you, those that mostly ignore me are not bad kids, just difficult to communicate with. Of course, the environments in which these teens have grown up are totally different. The friendly, thoughtful teens have supportive but disciplinary parents living together.

I'm drawn to the friendly teens and would help them with just about anything. However, I seldom say hello to the unfriendly teens any longer. Maybe I should, because they certainly could use a mentor, but they don't make it easy because they aren't sure how to accept kindness.

If one of your children shows a tendency toward an unappealing or impolite personality, it could be a difficult situation to deal with, or it could be a matter of learning some simple manners. Do what you must to correct this behavior. Incredibly, many parents don't really think about teaching manners; others aren't sure what good manners are. Instead, they take action only when they notice something—reacting rather than having a plan, an approach.

Manners must be taught when your children are young and reinforced constantly and consistently. Just think how often you see the following types of behavior: insubordination, interrupting, back talking, ignoring, not saying "thank you" or "excuse me," being late, not listening, and more. Actually, this type of behavior is not bad manners, but bad behavior. Having manners is good behavior with style. A young teen holding the door open for his mother is not only demonstrating good behavior, but good manners too.

Young people are not apt to know manners without some guidance and mentoring. You, Dad, are perfect for this mentoring role. Don't be lazy in correcting bad behavior or teaching good manners. Manners show respect for others and yourself. The power of children with good manners is underestimated, and the positive returns those manners bring are underappreciated. A respectful child is a likable child.

Respectfulness in your children is like a mirror; it is reflected back to you. When I was in high school, some of my friends had good manners and others did not. At that age, manners were not as necessary among us friends. But when we were around my mother or other adults, I expected my friends to be respectful and courteous to them. When I witnessed those who were not, it told me as much about their parents as it did about them.

Friends who did have good manners were always welcome in our house. Not only that, but they were given the benefit of any doubt and given second chances when honest mistakes were made. Adults returned that respectful treatment, giving me and my friends confidence and belief in ourselves.

DAD TIP:

People seem to have lost, or are ignoring, the fine art of teaching their children good manners. A wise man once said, "Good manners are never out of style." By helping your children learn to treat others well and respectfully, you are giving them tools that will serve them throughout their lives.

Those who were without good manners were not welcome and did not get the benefit of the doubt. Young people who have not been taught or who have not experienced an example of mannerly behavior don't know what a positive reaction it brings out in adults. Instead, they consider themselves to be misunderstood, unwelcome, and victimized. Envisioning themselves as victimized, these young people see a "them versus us" situation, tempting them to get even or rebel, and so is born another obstacle to mutual respect. The cycle can then spin out of control.

THE CHALLENGE OF LEARNING LIFE'S LESSONS

The best-learned lessons are those experienced firsthand. When your children are making mistakes, let them go as far as you can allow without them or someone else getting physically hurt, or before anything of real value gets damaged. The reason you do this is to help them learn to problem-solve, to learn consequences, to populate their memory banks with their own experiences, and to gain confidence; so you as a good father will not be overprotective or overbearing.

My wife, Kathy, pays close attention to the tags on the clothes she buys that tell her the type of fabric and washing instructions. When my older daughter, April, was old enough to have a job and earn some money, she naturally wanted to buy some clothes for herself. Kathy warned her to look at the labels and to try to stay away from certain fabrics, especially those that required dry cleaning. Well, this was a difficult lesson for April to grasp; Kathy would find April's new, nonwashable blouses in the laundry basket.

Of course, Kathy, being sensible, took them out and told April about them. But she never seemed to catch on. Finally, it was evident April wasn't getting the message. Kathy allowed one of April's less expensive, nonwashable blouses to be washed, and it came out misshapen and essentially ruined. April was upset when she saw what had happened to her new blouse, but that incident, along with knowing the cost of dry cleaning, put a clear stamp in her head about looking at labels when buying clothes.

A good father, a Dad, mentors *over the shoulder*, not in your face.

WHEN TO TAKE THE PATH OF LEAST RESISTANCE

The lazy kid, the unethical kid, the inexperienced kid, the painfully shy kid, the unmentored kid, and the well-adjusted kid—each has reasons to take the path of least resistance. But there is one huge difference. The well-adjusted kid does it intelligently, while the others use it as an excuse—here's why.

We learn in high school science that electricity takes the path of least resistance, as does water and all things in nature. In nature, this rule is the smart thing to do. For people, the path of least resistance is smart, but only when avoiding wasted energy toward a predetermined goal. Certainly when highway engineers build a road, they avoid the widest points of rivers and the highest mountains whenever they can. They have a destination in mind, and getting there most efficiently is the smartest and least expensive way to go. Eventually, they discover that narrow point in the river or the mountain foothills, and while they remain on the path of least resistance, there is still work to do to reach the goal. If they stop, the destination will never be reached. The path of least resistance does not mean there is no resistance or effort required.

Alternatively, the path of least resistance can also be something to avoid. Any worthwhile venture will require effort. Without mentoring, the lazy kid, the unethical kid, the inexperienced kid, or the painfully shy kid may take the easy way out to avoid work, embarrassment, or fear, or to rebel. Cheating on schoolwork, taking unchallenging classes, and playing video games in place of exercising are all easier paths to take, but these things will not take kids anywhere.

Professional golfers take as few strokes as possible to finish a round in a tournament. But when practicing, they stroke as many balls as they can to get better. The path of least resistance is beneficial or self-defeating, depending on the situation. Paying attention to when and why your children choose this path is a key to understanding them better.

INTELLIGENT PERSISTENCE

The difference between stubbornness and persistence is creativity. It takes a smart guy to find better ways to reach a goal. As I've said, sometimes that involves taking the path of least resistance.

When you simply teach a kid to be persistent, you are assuming quite a bit. They may think trying the same thing over and over will eventually work, even if it hasn't worked before. Once in a great while, it may work. But running into the proverbial brick wall until it gives way may not happen before you give way yourself.

Maybe there is a more creative way to your real goal that involves fewer struggles. Let's say your son wants to be a middle linebacker in a recreational football league, but he is not successful. Sure, he can put persistence into play by practicing hard, always concentrating, and listening to his coaches. If that works, then we have another success story. But if he continues to fail, it doesn't make sense for him to keep bashing into that brick wall. To find the success in football he is looking for, perhaps he would be better suited to play running back with its different set of skills.

Simply stated, stubbornness is fool's gold and persistence is pure gold, but persistence with creativity is gold currency, easily bartered or transferable to success. Try going around that brick wall with a little creativity. Running into it may just be foolish stubbornness.

THAT'S PART OF GROWING UP

There are some things in life that we all must learn as we grow up. A good father in the home can help his children learn these things successfully.

- Dealing with peer pressure is part of growing up. *A good father teaches his child how to deal with peer pressure, both good and bad.*
- Overcoming fear is part of growing up. *A good father will teach his child which fears are helpful and which are irrational.*

- Learning confidence is part of growing up. *A good father will teach confidence to his children with challenges that will tax them but won't exceed their abilities.*

- Understanding how your attitude affects your life is part of growing up. *A good father teaches how to not be a victim and supports good attitudes.*

- Knowing and learning the value of manners is part of growing up. *A good father teaches manners and how good manners will beget acceptance, allowances, and success.*

- Learning from consequences is part of growing up. *A good father teaches through consequences. Used properly, consequences are nothing more than lessons to correct ill behavior, and not punishment for punishment's sake.*

- Knowing when to take the path of least resistance is part of growing up. *A good father will teach his child that there are some efforts that can appropriately be minimized or avoided, while other efforts should never be cut short.*

The opposite is also true. Not having a good father in the home can be detrimental to a child's learning and growth. The following are things that do not have to be part of growing up if a child has a good father.

- Fitting in with whomever you can, however you can, or never fitting in at all is *not* part of growing up. *Looking for acceptance can become more important than having values. Not finding acceptance can lead to psychological issues.*

- Being afraid of the wrong things or being brave for the wrong reasons is *not* part of growing up. *Being afraid to ask for help will result in false bravado. Chest pounding does not signify bravery.*

- Never knowing real confidence is *not* part of growing up. *How can you be confident in the right areas when you don't have feedback from the right kind of people?*

- Having a "the world is against me" attitude is *not* part of growing *up. Being a victim places a person in a position of weakness, laziness, and rebellion.*

- Getting your way by force is *not* part of growing up. *When children don't know how to deal with people and have bad attitudes, they often resort to bullying, crime, or simple disrespect to steal or scare their way to what they want.*

- Always taking the path of least resistance to get by is *not* part of growing up. *Without mentoring, many children will take to the easy way out to avoid work, embarrassment, and fear—or to rebel.*

A good father, and a good mother, will guide their children as they grow up. The problem is that many parents had poor parenting role models themselves. *You raise your children the way you were raised, unless you make a conscious effort of doing things differently.* You are not likely to do this without training or mentoring.

YOUR ROAD MAP: CHAPTER 5

Start: Think hard about the challenges today's kids face.

Major Highway: Take notice of your children, their habits, their challenges, and their successes. Help them meet their fears, praise their efforts, and rejoice with them in their persistence.

On the Open Road: Imagine yourself as a young child or teen growing up today. What is different now from when you grew up? What challenges do your children face that you will need to watch for and help them meet?

Fifth Stop: Determine to be available, persistent, consistent, and comfortable with your children. Notice their habits. Know their fears. With your encouragement, expect them to meet and exceed the real and perceived challenges they face. Be there for them, but do not fight their battles for them.

CHAPTER 6

THE CHALLENGES OF FATHERING

"Obstacles to good fathering are often caused as the result of poor fathering of the father."
—Frank Pittman, *Man Enough*

There are many challenges to overcome to be an effective father. In the last chapter, we began a discussion of some of these challenges from the viewpoint of the child. *Your* first challenge is not to create obstacles on your own or to mishandle those that confront you.

THE CHALLENGE OF OBSTACLES

Obstacles to good fathering are many. These obstacles may include work, travel, illness, or perhaps more frustrating, a socially challenged or challenging child or an uncooperative mother. Sanford Braver et al. state that "40 percent of mothers reported that they had interfered with the father's visitation to punish their ex-spouse." However, when an obstacle involves your child, *you must overcome it*. To give in too easily underlines the real issue with too many fathers today: they don't really care. You can't blame another person for your not being involved with your children, even if it is an angry wife or ex-wife. As we teach our children, we can control our own actions. A Dad's action is to care.

THE CHALLENGE OF TIME

Creating appropriate time to nourish your children can be easy or difficult. If it strikes you that you could or should spend more time with your children, *do so*. It may be as easy as spending less time with your buddies or changing any activity that will shift priority to your child. Or it may *not* be as easy as "just doing it."

If you're a doctor, or in the military, time together may be precious. If so, then the time you have must be of a higher quality, focused on more direct involvement with your child. Phone calls, notes, and texts can be a way to remind your children how important they are to you.

If you spend every day "finding" yourself, or if working to feed your family commands all your attention, you may forget to enjoy the moments you will someday try to remember. Put reminders in your cell phone, on your wall calendar, anywhere and everywhere, to do something for or with your children each day, without annoying them. I do not mean buying them stuff. I mean being connected with them. Where there's a will, there is always a way.

THE CHALLENGE OF FEAR

Fear of the unknown, a topic we discussed earlier, is not only a symptom of childhood. Fear of the unknown burdens of fatherhood keeps some men from being the fathers they should be. Paradoxically, being a good father is as simple as realizing how easy it can be to become a good one. Just time, concern, love, and attention are enough. The unknowns are there for even the most successful fathers. Working at fathering does not necessarily have to be difficult, and it most definitely can be satisfying, especially since we are helping those we love.

If not already obvious, let's revisit why a Dad is so important. In a family, an involved father is a strong balance to the mother. Perhaps the mother may have more leverage, but the father may have more strength—or it could be reversed. Or while the mother may spend more time with the children than the father, he can make up for this with focused time. Mothers tend to shelter, while fathers tend to push. The mother exemplifies femininity while the father represents masculinity. Mothers are usually the predictable parents while fathers are often the wildcards, playing rougher, talking louder, and energizing their kids. Children flourish with exposure to both styles of parenting. Since the mother is more likely to be involved, only a father can provide the necessary balance of style, vision, perception, and indulgence, any of which may be a key to his children's success.

We all have potentials we are not aware of, including your children and you, the father. Sometimes it takes a father's challenge or his competitive nature for the untapped talents of his children to be discovered. What a waste it would be if the riches of your children lay hidden in streams of potential never panned for their gold.

Don't run away from a responsibility because you are uncertain or afraid. Being a father is just being yourself with a loving attitude toward your child. Being a father is being patient and being open to the help and ideas of others. When you do this, you are a true Dad.

Good fathers are real. They have to be themselves but be open *as* themselves. A good father cannot be described or defined in any one way. He is what he needs to be for his children and that can be different for all fathers. Usually that includes many of the specifics discussed in this book, such as being there for his children. But the real measure of a good Dad is in the subjective eyes of his children, and that's where it belongs.

DISCIPLINE, AUTHORITY, POWER, AND RESPECT

"Nothing is more despicable than respect based on fear."
—Albert Camus

As a father, do you know the differences and relationships between the terms *discipline, authority, power,* and *respect*? It's important that you do. *Discipline* involves enforcing proper behavior and skills. *Authority* is the proper placement or entitlement of power to someone. *Power* is the ability to have control over others. *Respect* is esteem or honor for one person from another. To discipline properly requires self-discipline, authority, power, and respect. Fathers and mothers have natural authority in most instances. Often, however, they lack power or respect. Any lack of respect you show your children will not earn respect in return. Without respect for your children, power can be devastating if they react out of fear. They are not learning what you want them to learn but likely something you don't want them to learn, and they stop respecting you as a father.

In *The Good Father*, Mark O'Connell states, "Paternal authority is among the easiest forms of authority to abuse." But he goes on to say that some men tend not to use their authority for fear of being abusive—while well meaning, this too can be a mistake. Again we bring in the notion of balance to this discussion. A father should have power and authority over his dependent children. The power should be in the background, understood but not necessary to discuss or display. If a man has to demonstrate his power as a father, he may have power but no respect. His authority, when paired with knowledge and caring, should be out in the open. You are the adult, the responsible teacher and example for your children. It is necessary for you and their mother to set expectations and correct unacceptable behavior. If you don't, many children carry their unacceptable behavior outside the family.

For example, if your daughter needs some correction, be sure not to minimize her. Minimizing her would be a misuse of your power and would be showing her no respect. Explaining to your son that his idea of jumping off the roof with his self-made parachute is not a good idea is teaching discipline and using your authority. To tell him he is the stupidest kid on earth would be shaming him, showing him no respect.

THE CHALLENGE OF DISCIPLINE

Discipline can indicate restraint or punishment. Both forms of discipline teach respect, manners, propriety, and self-control. One of your most important duties as a parent is to teach discipline (restraint) and to employ discipline (punishment). In these cases, be your children's father; do not try to be their friend.

You may have heard that warning before, but you need to really think about what it means.

Children need authority figures to keep them in check, especially before they have developed their sense of right and wrong. Don't be afraid of losing favor with them, even if you are "competing" with their mother for time and attention. (By the way, this competition should never occur.) Right is right, and misleading your children by overlooking indiscretions is a big mistake. Point out to them how to behave in a more proper manner.

Your children will be clever in challenging your authority, choosing situations where you are disadvantaged, such as throwing a tantrum in public or pitting mother against father. You have to be assertive in setting standards that address such situations ahead of time.

It is also possible you have contributed to the discipline issues. Reflect on the possibility that your children have seen their misbehavior work when they've worn you down and gotten what they wanted. As much as is practical, you must ignore inappropriate behavior designed to get your attention, while praising, as much as possible, good behavior. Whining and pouting will not last long if you ignore it. Acknowledging good behavior is a positive way to reinforce it.

THE CHALLENGE OF EVERYDAY LIFE

Things often go wrong. There are days when plans don't always work out and people are unkind; when the weather is bad and the traffic worse; when you have a headache and your boss passes you up for an important project.

Do you want to listen to everyone's problems and complaints when you get home? *Not me!* you say to yourself. What you want to do is go hide while the kids bang on your cave door and your wife yells that she's the one who needs a break—and she's right. But you want to gather yourself so you don't take your frustrations out on the family. It's a tough situation, but you must try to find a way to keep your cool.

You are not the only one who has bad days. Perhaps your son or daughter didn't make the soccer team, or they just argued with a good friend. Or worse, they may not be popular at school and are having trouble dealing with bullies, or they just received a disappointing report card. It is vital not to ignore your children's problems just because you are buried in your own.

When these bad days happen, fathers, mothers, and children need to combat the resulting bad feelings or lousy attitudes. There are techniques and tools to help us overcome our down periods. Maybe a pep talk in the mirror or an inspirational quote works for you, or a friend (maybe your own Dad) who will listen to you.

Sometimes a brisk game of basketball or a long walk will do wonders. I remember once screaming into a pillow and, strangely, it seemed to help. It may be just knowing that, in time, the rough day will pass. Shaking off the excess negative energy will help keep you or your child from internalizing the problem. It is important to find what techniques work for you and to suggest techniques to your children.

If you have a child who seems unable to handle misfortune, do not push it under the rug. Do what you can to keep this attitude from becoming a potentially serious problem. Discounting deeper psychological reasons, the odds of your child *not* being able to rebound are remote with the safety net of your love and comfort. But get professional help for your child if necessary. To understand emotions, how to interpret them, and how to react, I suggest reading *Life Energy* by John Diamond.

THE CHALLENGE OF PERSONALITY

"Men are respectable only as they respect."
—Ralph Waldo Emerson

The type of people we are can make parenting a challenge. If we are anxious, we can overreact by trying to protect our children from every possible threat. If we are cavalier about life, we may not protect them enough. If we are free spirits, then discipline may be an issue. If we are authoritarian and stifle our children, then they may lose their creativity or react to us in a negative way.

The only antidote to fight our *own* personality issues is an open mind. We must understand ourselves as men before we can understand our actions. We need to be careful not to take criticism of our fathering lightly or angrily. This will take a lot of courage, but with an open mind, it can help us understand ourselves and our children.

THE CHALLENGE OF IMAGE

Never be discouraged by not being perfect. Just as our children are not without fault, neither are we as parents. No one is asking you to be Ward Cleaver or Sheriff Andy Taylor, successful TV fathers of the past. Be real, not like the hero in the movies, the athlete in the stadium, or the guy next door. It doesn't matter if you're clumsy, uneducated, unathletic, or blind. Your thoughtfulness, attention, love, and kindness are what count.

We cannot be perfect because that is not how life works. So it is vital to remember you are allowed to make mistakes. When you make a mistake, you can learn from it, make it good, say you're sorry, or all of the above.

Never give up trying to do the right thing for your children, whether that is giving more attention or less. Learn what works and what doesn't work. You are a person, not a robot. The biggest mistake you'll ever make is not learning from the inevitable mistakes—because mistakes are the best teacher you'll ever have.

THE CHALLENGE OF BEING A GOOD EXAMPLE

> *"Sometimes the poorest man leaves his children the richest inheritance."*
>
> —Ruth E. Renkel

Of course it helps if, as a mentor, you are a good example. It's not that children don't learn good things from bad examples—they certainly do. But how they react to that example is something you don't want to leave to chance.

Perhaps your angry demeanor, impatience, or even rudeness will teach them they would never want to be like you. Is that what you want? Or they may be blind to those faults because of their need for your attention and approval and, unknowingly to them, follow your faulty examples. Is that what you want? Put simply, when you are a bad example, they will either dislike you or be ashamed of you, or you will mislead them into following your bad behavior throughout their lives.

THE CHALLENGE OF ASKING FOR HELP

Men are always accused of being averse to asking for directions. This is often true, and we also see this in parenting. A foundational truth of not only fathering but also parenting in general is to admit you don't know everything about raising kids and neither you nor your children are models of perfection. Don't be too proud or too lazy to get your children help when you and their mother can't help them yourselves.

Did you know that kids, usually boys, are sometimes expelled from preschool? I asked my parent-educator wife, Kathy, why this happens.

She said that boys can be developmentally behind in the ability to express themselves verbally. If this problem is ignored, it can result in their frustration being expressed through violence.

Kathy said that often parent educators test children and find they are not where they should be in their ability to socialize. Being behind in verbal skills is an example of this. Many parents of these children ignore an educator's advice or choose not to believe it. The result of their pride or ignorance can be detrimental to the child's development. Never hesitate to get your children help from experts when they need it. When developmental issues are addressed early enough, children can put any correctable issues behind them and keep pace with their peers.

RISK FACTORS OF FATHERHOOD

Life is a challenge. And how boring would life be without these challenges? Some we avoid, some we welcome, and many come without invitation. The challenge of being a father can fall into any of these categories.

Challenges can be analyzed by your likelihood of meeting them and by the consequences if you do not. As a systems engineer in my civilian career, I studied risk. Risk analysis is not limited to engineering, gambling, or finance—we see it in everyday life as well. The measure of risk is based on two factors: one is the likelihood that a bad (or good) outcome will occur, and the other is the consequence if it does. Let's look at risk from a fatherly viewpoint and examine your likelihood of being a good Dad. We have already discussed the consequences of good and bad fathering.

How well you do as a father depends on so many things: how you were brought up, how much you care about your child or fatherhood in general, how much natural fathering instinct you are fortunate enough to have. Do you like kids? How well do you get along with the child's mother? Are you willing to learn? Do you have patience, empathy, and understanding? Do you have a sense of humor? These are just some of the variables that, when explored, predict how well you will do as a Dad.

THE CONSEQUENCES OF POOR FATHERING ARE DISASTROUS

"Men who have lost their children [through emotional distance] hide a horrible pain—one that they may go to great lengths to mask from themselves and others."
—Mark Bryan, *The Prodigal Father*

A consequence in itself is not necessarily bad, but the consequence of poor or absent fathering is almost always negative. Both statistics and common experience prove this. Healthy children come from healthy parenting. We can build a healthier society, one child at a time. We have but one chance to help our children create a positive impact on society.

What I hope to increase is the number of good fathers by promoting awareness and mentoring. What I have not yet figured out is how to get an unaware, uncaring, irresponsible father to pay attention to the discussions, techniques, and goals of fatherhood. It is a "chicken or egg" problem. Which comes first, a good Dad, interested in learning proven fathering skills, or learning proven fathering skills, then becoming a good Dad? A caring father is interested in improving his fatherly skills; he is not perfect, but for our society, he is not the real problem.

The men and boys who don't care about the children they father do not care to educate themselves on this topic. Those are the very men who need their ignorance reversed, somehow, for the good of their children and society.

But between the conscientious father and the hopeless father is the father in the middle. He is the one who wants to care but is unsure of his ability. Or he was raised in an environment where fatherly love was not emphasized. It is my hope that their wives, girlfriends, mothers, grandmothers, sisters, brothers, aunts, uncles, friends, clergy, and others will emphasize the importance of their fathering, especially their potential to positively impact the lives of their children—more potential than anyone else on earth, except their mother.

We already know what it takes to be a father. At the very least, it takes hormones and carelessness. The real test is this: Will we learn what it takes to be a Dad? To increase your enthusiasm for learning to be a better Dad, knowing the consequences of *not* being a good father may help you. And the more we understand these personal and social implications, the more we realize how disastrous the consequences can be. Poor education, ill health, mental instability, crime, poverty, dependence on welfare, more children without fathers—these can all be consequences of poor fathering. We can increase the likelihood of good fathering, but it is doubtful that we can significantly decrease the consequences of poor fathering.

The challenges of fathering become more complex when the mix of personalities we all face come together in a family. We will discuss this topic in the next chapter.

YOUR ROAD MAP: CHAPTER 6

Start: Never discount the challenges of fathering and becoming a good Dad. It's hard work, but well worth your effort.

Major Highway: We teach our children to meet their challenges head-on, with our support and guidance. Likewise, as Dads we sometimes need support and guidance as we meet the challenges of fatherhood. Never be afraid to ask for help. You have unlimited potential.

On the Open Road: Imagine how you would solve a friend's fathering challenges. Then look at your own obstacles and try to see them from another's point of view. Taking this "other" view of the challenges you face may give you new perspective and fodder for discussion with your friends who are Dads.

Sixth Stop: Time, resources, patience, knowledge, instinct—all can be challenges to fatherhood. Take the time to think about these and the other challenges presented in this book, and if they pertain to you, come up with at least one new action or solution you will try as you meet your fathering challenges head-on.

CHAPTER 7

THE CHALLENGES OF THE FAMILY

"There are no adequate substitutes for father, mother, and children bound together in a loving commitment to nurture and protect. No government, no matter how well-intentioned, can take the place of the family in the scheme of things."

—Gerald Ford, thirty-eighth president of the United States

It's difficult to define a core family anymore. I would like to define it as a mother, a father, and their children. Many would object to this traditional view, and I would not blame them. Families come in different shapes and sizes, and many of those families do not have a father involved, at least in an everyday sense. I applaud families of all types, including single-parent families, grandparent families, mixed families, childless families, and any other family that works together to be successful. These families are often what they want, or have, to be.

But I think the optimal family for child rearing comprises a mother, a father, and their children. Overall, that is the best and classic scenario for raising healthy children. Opinions aside, statistics overwhelmingly bear this out.

However, in 2010 single parents accounted for around 27 percent of family households with children under the age of 18, and 80 percent of those households were headed by women. For black children, the single-parent figure is 52 percent (NFI). These numbers are growing. With that introduction, I speak of the family atmosphere where there is a father involved, whether or not he lives with his children.

A FAMILY IS A TEAM

One of the true basics of fatherhood is to realize your family is a team. A successful team has a system, or way of doing things, that every member of the team can believe in. This is more important than the quality of the environment itself.

By and large, buy-in (acceptance) comes from a fair, flexible, workable, and believable system. Sometimes, however, a good system—a good plan—is not enough. You must really sell your plan and get total commitment for your system to work. In your work environment, for example, it would be foolish to simply throw a plan out there and say, "Just go do it!" (although it happens).

DAD TIP:

Your family's "rules of living" are like a team's game plan. Everyone on the team—or in the family—must understand the plan, how people work together, what is allowed and not allowed, and what each person can expect of the others. It's the system under which the team or family operates.

Whether or not you as a dad live with your family, your interactions with your children must follow the game plan. Everyone needs to know what to expect.

The same can be said for family life. In a family, a system (a plan or an agreement) can be a set of rules, beliefs, or standards. Most of the time these are never written down, but they should be clear. They are held and expressed by the mother and father in their actions and reactions.

As a parent, you give direction, answer questions, and make corrections—sometimes nonverbally. The system you represent is taken in and judged by your children in great detail. Probably the first thing they are looking for is consistency. They may not be looking for it consciously, but they will definitely notice whether or not it is there. Without consistency, there is no system; there is only chaos. Unfortunately, the most consistent trait of many parents is their inconsistency.

> **DAD TIP:**
> *Every family unit must have consistency at its core. Your family is a team, and your team members must understand the rules. As a parent, especially as a father, your role is to bring order from the world's chaos. You must help your child understand that home—the place of safety and love—is always there, always to be depended upon.*

Any family system should include the following:

- Encouragement of the child's independence, dreams, and individuality.
- Open communication between parents and children, listening to each other's points of view. Parents explain their decisions, and children are respectful when giving their opinions and wishes. Parents likewise listen to their children's reasoning and help them form good reasoning skills.
- Fair expectations for both children and parents—children should expect clear standards set by their parents, and parents should expect age-appropriate, mature behavior from their children.
- Enforcement of rules and standards, being firm and using consequences when necessary.

- If parents are not living together, for the good of the children the system must span both households and be consistent.

FATHERHOOD VERSUS MOTHERHOOD

Mothers are the true heroes of this world. Their loyalty, dedication, sacrifices, never-ending worry, and backbreaking, unglamorous work given for the well-being of their children and families can never be overestimated. Mothers, with few exceptions, can be trusted to do their best for their children. Nature has put women, as a whole, on an instinctive path in their nurturing role.

The same cannot be said for men. Most males consider nurturing as a more natural talent for women. We fathers also nurture, but we need to be reminded, and sometimes taught, how important we are. And we often need mentoring to do it well. Men are different from women, which is why we need to be involved in the lives of our children.

Dads bring a different perspective to the home environment. We love differently from the women in our children's lives. We seek to offer consistency, firmness, strength, and love in ways only Dads can bring.

As David Popenoe wrote in *Life Without Father*, "Early bonding between father and child is strongly associated with a father's later desire to want to maintain contact with that child. . . . Father care, more than mother care, is learned behavior."

Parenting is a team effort. Moms parent in a mother's way and Dads parent in a father's way—a perfect complement, like a nut and a bolt. My mother sheltered me from my fears. My father, when he was around, made me face them. My mom made us fried chicken with mashed potatoes and corn, while my dad surprised us with White Castle hamburgers. My mom was gentle and soft-spoken, but my dad had a rough beard and strong hands and wore flannel shirts.

I liked having both a mother and a father with their different styles and outlooks. When my father was no longer around, I missed his presence more than I knew. One reason I didn't realize how much I was missing is because my first reaction was relief. I was relieved that the constant conflict between my mom and dad no longer lurked around every corner. No longer was there the daily dread that conflict would erupt. The relative tranquility and lack of the fear I felt in my father's absence was a welcome aspect of my father's leaving our family. But there was most certainly a downside.

THE CHALLENGE OF DEFINING YOUR ROLE

Certainly Dads are not meant to take the place of Moms. There are likely *more* things that only a mother can do compared with things only a father can do—but that is not the point. What good would a sailboat be without a sail? What good is a sail without a boat? Often the mother is the boat and the father the sail.

Dads should change a diaper, but it's not necessary to be a good Dad. It's nice when a Dad combs his daughter's hair, but is he a bad father if he doesn't do so? To do these things would be perfectly normal for some Dads but may put other Dads off a bit. Having a "caveman mentality"—men hunt and provide, women take care of domestic issues—doesn't always equate to being a bad Dad. Unnecessary pressure to do certain tasks should be weighed against the good and necessary things he does otherwise as a father.

Each parent's role is a family issue that needs reflection, conversation, and likely compromise. We need to remember it is the child who is important, not rigid equality in parental duties. Ideally and logically, a child needs a functioning mother and father, not parents who don't know their roles.

Fathers need to be comfortable and confident, or they may fail in their role. A man must be himself as a father because what comes naturally comes easiest. Of course, he must subdue certain temperaments like being aloof, grouchy, or too busy. We all have our moments of being less than perfect, and that's okay, but we must always try to be better.

For fathering to be natural, we only have to be ourselves. If you are a fisherman, take your kids fishing. If you're a NASCAR fan, go to a race. If you like spectator sports, take them to a ball game. Teach them woodworking if that's what you know best. Read with them if you like to read. Just be actively involved with your kids.

DAD TIP:

Men tend to either overthink or underthink their fathering roles and abilities. The key is to be yourself, love your child, and work with your child's mother to keep expectations consistent.

When necessary, a father's role can be replaced by another male mentor. But that will only be a partial solution to a problem. A replacement for a father should never be a choice—only a necessity—because, all things being equal, how can a male mentor be as good as the real father? Rarely would another male have as profound or as long lasting a relationship as a biological father. It is simply not as natural a bond, even when volunteers for this important role are available, approachable, and capable. Nevertheless, God bless male role models who try to help fatherless children, especially boys who will someday be fathers—hopefully Dads—themselves.

THE CHALLENGE OF CLEAR COMMUNICATION BETWEEN PARENTS

Different parental roles require coordination. No one can read another person's mind. If parents cannot communicate, it can be especially hurtful to your children. Poor communication can cause assumptions, and assumptions can cause grave mistakes. Misunderstandings can grow into faultfinding. Soon your family system is not functioning well, and no one, most of all the children, can be at ease.

This can be especially true when the parents don't live with each other. There have been numerous accounts of kids not being picked up by a parent because the other parent hasn't properly and distinctly handed off the responsibility. If not found by someone else, these children could be left helpless for hours.

This is just one simple example of the need for parent-to-parent communication and coordination. Who's dropping them off? Who's picking them up? Feeding, sleeping, medicine, discipline, schoolwork, and friends are just some of the topics that, if not coordinated, can cause problems ranging from arguments to tragic mishaps. If you have disagreements about these issues, don't allow them to cause confusion regarding your children's health and safety.

Long-term issues are also extremely important to coordinate with your child's mother. What are your observations about your child's needs and behavior? Have you discussed their education? What do you see as your responsibilities in the future? Do you know your child's desires, concerns, and goals? Fathers, be on the same page as your children's mother when it involves your children.

THE CHALLENGE OF BALANCING YOUR ATTENTION

"I never thought what my philosophy is, but it has to be balance in everything you do."

—Abdullah A. Badawi

Balancing attention among your children is vitally important. By this I don't mean thirty minutes for each kid per night. I mean balancing attention according to their changing needs. Sometimes you need to invest more in the neediest kid. Not the kid who whines the most, mind you, but the neediest kid—often the neediest one is the quietest one. But while you're helping one child, look in your rearview mirror to check on the others.

A parent must never show favoritism for one child over the others. If your spouse or children accuse you of this, don't dismiss it. It may not be true, but their perception means something is not right.

Children often misbehave or rebel to gain attention. Their needs may be an indication of your imbalance as a parent. Maybe you haven't been giving them the guidance or love they need. When you rebalance, they will hopefully readjust, and the misbehaving and rebelling will go away. But be careful not to associate your positive change with their negative behavior, or you may inadvertently reinforce the rebellious behavior and become their hostage. Put simply, don't react to tantrums or threats.

Overt rebellion is revealing, but less obvious behavior can also reveal a lot. You may notice that your son or daughter is too withdrawn or unable to be alone. They could be addicted to video games, food, comic books, or something much worse.

Some children cry too easily while others never cry. Others seem to live in a fantasy world while others have no imagination. None of these traits in moderation are bad, but give them your attention and seek ways to get your children out of any ruts they may be trapped in.

Parenting, unfortunately, is not 'one size fits all.' Since each child is unique, a technique that works with one child may not work for another. You also must not ignore one child's undesirable character traits while obsessing over the minor indiscretions of another. It will always be a balancing act. Sometimes you will wobble. Don't be discouraged.

DAD TIP:

Balance is a tricky thing, as anyone who has ever learned to ride a bike knows. You have to pay attention to what you are doing or you might lose your balance or veer off your desired path. As a Dad, you must be personally balanced to do your fathering well, to notice what each child needs. And you must also balance your time with your children based on their current needs. It's not a matter of equal time; it's a matter of focused parenting.

In Madelyn Swift's book *Discipline for Life: Getting It Right with Children*, she discusses the "Law of the Harvest"—you reap what you sow.

How you treat your children will create expectations in them. If you continually over-reward your children for every good deed or behavior, as they grow older they will make choices based on how they will benefit. Life choices become a mental exercise in "how can I make this work for me?" This kind of thinking feeds the child's ego and tends to separate them from the greater good. Descriptive terms such as spoiled and manipulative come to mind.

On the other hand, if you always over-punish your children for behavior undesirable to you or someone else, they can become resentful and bitter. They avoid punishment not by behaving properly, but by doing what they can to not get caught.

Where over-rewarded children think only of themselves, over-punished children work against everyone. If you try to control your children too much, they learn that the way to influence others is to be in control. And how do people control others? Most often it is by manipulation and abuse of power.

THE CHALLENGE OF REALITY AND SUPPORT

"Parents of young children should realize that few people, and maybe no one, will find their children as enchanting as they do."
—Barbara Walters

I'm sure many grandparents would disagree with Ms. Walters. But it is largely true. Our children are so special to us, but don't push them upon others. They are special in the context that they are our responsibility to bring up as respectful children and respected adults. They are special because we love them. They are special because they are a reflection of us and our values, of our hopes for them and their families to come. They are each special as one of God's beings.

Absolutely, your children are special. But your child is not more special than anyone else's child. You must keep this perspective, both for you and for them. As loving parents, this is admittedly difficult (and as a grandfather now, I admit it is even more difficult to remember).

Teach your kids to compete and compete hard, but also to compete fairly. Competition is a healthy and fun part of life. Kids learn so much about themselves, and they strengthen their brains and bodies.

However, consider these circumstances. If your daughter is in a "fun" softball league, don't think she should play more because she is a better player. The intent of "for-fun" leagues is for all to play, learn, and have fun. On the other hand, if she is in a competitive league, don't expect her to play as often if she is not one of the best players. The intent in competitive leagues is to win.

Your children are special to you, but on a team, even though all the players should be equal in opportunity, they will not be equal in talent or performance. Often we are blind to their true talent level because of our desire to see them do well.

Truly special children care for others as much as themselves. My ultimate disappointment as a father would have been if I had seen any of my kids mistreat someone. Thankfully, I never witnessed them being unkind (except to each other, as siblings sometimes do), and I'm so proud that each of my three children has gone out of their way to be kind to those who need kindness the most.

DAD TIP:

Raising balanced children will bring you a world of pleasure. When you see your daughter being kind to the kid at school whom nobody likes, when you see your son help another kid in need, you are viewing what your adult children could be like. When a Dad recognizes these positive traits, he should reinforce them, thus encouraging childhood behaviors to become permanent character traits. Balance in the family system is your key.

A friend of mine has a nine-year-old daughter who is the absolute apple of his eye. She receives special treatment in all the right ways. She was read to as a little girl. She was given riding lessons, which gave her a love of animals and a healthy hobby. She was sent to the best school available for her slight learning disability. She keeps in touch with extended family members who live out of state, people who never forget her.

This little girl is well grounded. She has been taught to love animals and people. She thinks of others and befriends those who need friends. She is special because she doesn't think of herself as special outside of her family.

Kids who have been pumped up by their parents as elite or gifted or semi-royalty can be absolute snobs. They may be special or talented in some way, but when they think they are special above others, their attitudes can be downright obnoxious. Egotistical children are not balanced because their parents have not raised them in a balanced fashion.

THE CHALLENGE OF INFLUENCE

Parents provide their children's culture. A culture is learned or passed on by lessons, observation, and symbols. DNA determines that you'll have red hair and a tendency toward high blood pressure; culture is responsible, at a minimum, for your religious beliefs, family traditions, and social characteristics.

You will be Asian if your parents are Asian, and you will likely be Mormon if the people who raise you are Mormon. One is biological, and the other is cultural. While no one can change your DNA, your culture is malleable. If a Polish-Catholic infant boy is raised by a German-Jewish family, his genes are still Polish and male, but his culture will teach him to speak German, not Polish, and he will most likely attend a synagogue rather than a church.

Adoption and the work of missionaries are perfect examples of the influence of culture. Your culture could be Latin, European, or African; it could be Christian, Muslim, or Jewish; you could live in a city, a small town, or a rural area; your family could be close-knit, diverse, or economically deprived. Many of us have similar cultures, but few have identical cultures, especially at the family level.

Families are mini-cultures within larger cultures, and they have a tremendous influence on the lives of their members. Families without effective fathers are mini-cultures that are out of balance, where just surviving or getting by takes up everyone's energy, often without the vision of a better life. A family with an ineffective or absent father has no choice but to move on without him. This often spawns a culture of despair and negativity, and too few escape its trap.

NATURE VERSUS NURTURE

There has been a longtime debate regarding the impacts of nature versus nurture. The famous racehorse Seabiscuit was a Thoroughbred by nature, but nurturing made him a champion. Even though I strongly advocate nurturing by fathers, there is no denying the powerful impact that nature has on our children. Studies involving twins separated at birth reveal amazingly similar characteristics that can only be explained by nature. We also speak of our own personalities, actions, reactions, and inner selves as our "nature," but this is different from the biological nature referred to here.

My nurturing was virtually the same as my siblings', yet my nature was different. My siblings would tell you I was the oddball in our family. My nature was not better or worse, but it was different and helped me come to a different place in my life.

There's no denying that some wonderfully nurturing parents have had troubled children while many amazingly successful people were raised without present or functional parents. So why bother with nurturing?

I subscribe to the "Eighty-Percent Rule." Eighty percent of children with ineffective parents will be significantly troubled, and eighty percent of children with effective parents will be relatively well adjusted. The remaining twenty percent in each case defy the odds.

THE CHALLENGE OF DIVERSITY AND COOPERATION

To be in a diverse and cooperative society, we must learn how to accept differences in thought, be open to new approaches to problems, and cooperate with each other to come to the best solution for all. This type of problem solving requires experience. When our children learn that they cannot comfortably survive in society alone, they appreciate the efforts of others and want to contribute in their own way. This is the essence of diversity and cooperation.

We must all realize we are dependent on others, as they are dependent on us. We are at once self-reliant and dependent. I may be responsible to get to work on time, but I may also be dependent on the public transportation system. If I have an important meeting or presentation in the morning, I might need to have a backup plan.

An example of this, put into the context of your children, will fascinate them and get them thinking about things they might not consider on their own:

> When you wake up in the morning and rub the sleep from your eyes, you go to eat breakfast made by Mom or Dad. Your breakfast was made possible by hardworking farmers who raised the cows and pigs to make your milk and sausage and grew the grains that make your cereal. Truck drivers often drive overnight to take these farm items to stores run by business people who understand supply and demand—that is, what people want and when they want it. When you get dressed, your clothes may have been created by people who have a knack for design and made by garment workers across the ocean who speak a different language.
>
> Your school bus is driven by a person who must be very responsible for all the children on board. The bus was designed by engineers who had to go to school and study very hard to do what they do, and it was built by men and women who are good with their hands. These people work in build-

ings designed by architects and built by ironworkers and carpenters. The roads you travel on were paid for by taxes all working people pay, with the help of politicians who ask for the road construction funds that pay construction workers to lay the concrete or asphalt and make necessary repairs.

So, before you even get to school, you will have been helped by farmers, truck drivers, business people, designers, bus drivers, engineers, factory workers, architects, ironworkers, carpenters, taxpayers, politicians, construction workers, and countless others we have forgotten or don't know about. While getting to school on time is your responsibility, you are dependent on so many others to do so. If those you depend on aren't reliable, then you are responsible to find another way that helps you meet your commitments.

At this point, you could let your child take over and continue telling the story about their day. The lesson is obvious. All of us experience the benefits of diversity and cooperation every day.

If you put a hip-hop city boy, a suburban middle-class girl, and a farm boy in a room together, they are less likely to be comfortable with each other than with those in their own crowd. Now let's say they were challenged to learn to rock climb in order to compete with another group. Each person in our trio must learn a skill and depend on each other or the group will fail. Their combined talents and diverse experiences will serve them better than having similar backgrounds. Dependency on each other and their increased teamwork will significantly boost their chances of becoming friends. Experiences are the best teachers, especially when challenges exist and teamwork is required.

Although families tend to be culturally homogeneous, diversity still exists with differences in age, gender, attitudes, talents, and inclinations. Just like the rock-climbing team, if a family is taught to work together, everyone will benefit.

A BALANCED FAMILY: DIVERSITY WITH COOPERATION

A father is not just important to each of his children, but to his family as a whole. This may be an obvious statement, but it may not be obvious why.

Families can be described in terms of two characteristics: diversity and tendency to cooperate. A family's *diversity* is the degree to which family members differ from one another in personality and role, and where each has the freedom and ability to be who they are without prejudice and without being smothered.

A family's *tendency to cooperate* refers to the extent to which each member of the family communicates and enhances one another's goals through support and understanding. A family that is only diverse will be chaotic, and one that is only cooperative will be smothering. When a family is diverse and cooperative, it is functional (or at least less dysfunctional than most families).

A family raised by a mother alone may have difficulty in these terms. A mother may be great at allowing or encouraging diversity among her children, but she may not have the time, energy, or inclination to encourage cooperation among them. On the other hand, she may concentrate on family organization and cooperation, thereby limiting her ability to support diversity. Or she may attempt a balance of both, but not have the time or ability to succeed. The same would be true of a father raising his family on his own. To achieve a perfect balance of diversity and cooperation alone would take a special parent indeed.

A family with both an involved father and an involved mother allows for each parent to assume roles which best complement each other. A father can ensure that his children have their own dreams and can encourage them to achieve those goals, while the mother can set the example for the family members to love and encourage each other. Or it can be the other way around.

DAD TIP:

True Dads can see that diversity and cooperation are important in their families and to their children. Men who are little more than biological fathers can lack this understanding. Any child raised in an environment where diversity and cooperation are balanced is fortunate indeed. Dads who interact with their children in a diverse and cooperative family system can help prepare their children for eventually living outside the safe confines of the family.

Each parent will most likely contribute to creating both diversity and cooperation. Allowing diversity, however, has limits if respect, the law, or decency is threatened, and cooperation has limits if coddling and giving in too easily occur. We see, then, that not only is there a need for balance between diversity and cooperation, but balance also *within* diversity and cooperation. No one said it would be easy being a parent.

OUT OF BALANCE: FAMILIES WHERE DIVERSITY TRUMPS COOPERATION

My childhood family would have been described as diverse yet uncooperative. Our family, therefore, was chaotic. I always knew we were chaotic, but now I know a bit about why. The diversity was out of control in that each child was afforded the opportunity, through lack of control, to push the limits of social order. Diversity can occur without control, but cooperation cannot. Without my father to help, the lack of control did not allow for time to encourage or develop talent, or to teach disciplined cooperation.

By the time all four Smith brothers and two Smith sisters reached eighteen years of age, there was only one high school diploma, a few minor arrests for truancy and bad behavior, and four out-of-wedlock children, with more kids, divorces, and trouble on the way. There are challenges in this style of family, and little or no support. A solely diverse family often produces independent-minded but troubled individuals.

OUT OF BALANCE: FAMILIES WHERE COOPERATION TRUMPS DIVERSITY

A cooperative family with no diversity in thought is a self-smothering family. The family members are happy in their own little world, supporting what each other does mostly because it is what they would do. Family members rationalize for each other, and they band together when anyone takes action, right or wrong, against their own. Their cooperation usually goes beyond the border of extreme coddling. There is no chaos here. To anyone outside the family, there is nothing interesting going on. There is support in this style of family, but little or no challenge.

Individuals from highly cooperative-only families are usually not independent, nor are they contributors to society. I have a friend from this type of family. He lived with his parents until they died and now lives with his sister and her husband in their parents' house. He does function successfully out of the home for the most part, but he is highly sensitive to criticism and is intolerant of views different from those he was raised with. At home, his complaints are listened to with sympathy by his sister and brother-in-law. He loves the reassurance of his family and is not interested in changing his situation. My friend is a nice, generous person, but he must be treated with tender care, for if he perceives any mistreatment, he sees himself as a victim and tends to brood.

THE CHALLENGE OF TOLERANCE

"The weak can never forgive. Forgiveness is the attribute of the strong."
—Mahatma Gandhi

A family, especially a predominantly diverse family, will experience conflict when viewpoints, wants, and needs collide. What a diverse and cooperative family can do is be patient and tolerant. Just tolerating the tolerable will prevent unnecessary tension.

Yet too many families are torn because of petty intolerances among family members. Some things we are intolerant of are simply our own issue, not our spouse's and not our children's. Your petty intolerance should not have to be tolerated by your family.

When the intolerance is between a husband and wife, the home atmosphere can be uncomfortable or frightening for all, especially the children. A wife can tolerate her husband's fanatic interest in sports, but she shouldn't have to tolerate his lack of concern for her or their children.

DAD TIP:

Every relationship and every family will have moments where one person cannot tolerate another's actions. That is normal. What is not normal is when that intolerance—or overtolerance of inappropriate behavior— becomes the norm. From unresolved intolerance or overtolerance comes contempt, argument, disappointment, fear, and sadness—in short, a totally imbalanced family system.

I could suggest what to tolerate and what not to tolerate, but that would be inappropriate and assuming of me because every family is different. There are things we don't tolerate and darn well shouldn't. But approach intolerable behavior in a way that doesn't make the situation worse. What's important is to just be aware of the virtue of having patience and being tolerant. Think before you react. Sometimes it is simply that awareness that prevents, solves, or resolves a problem.

ADDRESSING THE CHALLENGES

We've addressed the challenges of being a kid, the challenges of being a father, and the challenges of the family as a whole. Now we move on to the actions a father can take to meet those challenges. In Chapter 1, "The Power of Fatherhood," I introduced the Pyramid of Dadhood: being present is the foundation, providing love and comfort is built on that, and at the pinnacle, teaching and nurturing. In the next chapter, we start by discussing just how important the base of this fathering pyramid is—in other words, how important your presence is to your children.

YOUR ROAD MAP: CHAPTER 7

Start: Realize there are major challenges that all parents face, but parenting is even more difficult when the mother and father do not live in the same household.

Major Highway: Talk with your children's mother. Discuss the family system that will work best for you and for your children. Take into account the importance of balance, consistency, and the family model you wish to build.

On the Open Road: Imagine what our country and our world could be like if all fathers and mothers worked together on loving and consistent parenting. What could happen if all parents taught and exemplified cooperation and acceptance of diversity? What if intolerance and over-tolerance of diversity were not in play? What kind of balance could be achieved?

Seventh Stop: Think about the many challenges of parents working together to raise their children. Ask yourself what you can do to address the challenges of today's families, and make your own family—no matter how it is composed—stronger, more accepting of diversity, more cooperative, and better balanced.

THE
PYRAMID OF
DADHOOD

CHAPTER 8

BE THERE!

"If fathers who fear fathering and run away from it could only see how little fathering is enough. Mostly, the father just needs to be there."

—Frank Pittman, *Man Enough*

Don't ever talk yourself out of being there for your kids. Your involvement or your absence will have an enormous impact on your children. They want you there with them, and if you feel the same way, it will allow miracles to occur that could have been nightmares. Your greatest leverage and influence is when your children are young; you need to be there for them in body and spirit. This is the base of the Pyramid of Dadhood.

More men would be much more involved if they realized the contribution they make to their children's well-being. Our society struggles to recognize the profound influence of fatherhood and award credit when and where it is due. Or maybe there's just a lack of emphasis on the fatherly role.

Further, while any father-child time is important, what really makes its mark is the quality, real devotion, amount of listening, and caring shared during that time. Often, just being around your children will encourage these things.

You don't have to be in a serious discussion or joking with them all the time. It's more of an attitude, an invisible positive vibration you send out. You'll find that the more you honestly work at it, the better Dad you'll be, the more you will enjoy it, and the better your children will react to your direction. You will be proud of what you have accomplished as a Dad, and this satisfaction will far outweigh that which you feel when you succeed at work or enjoy time with your friends.

REALLY BEING THERE!

> *"Woody Allen once said that 80 percent of success is just show-*
> *ing up. With apologies to Woody, I would amend that statement*
> *to read that 99 percent of parenting consists of just being there."*
> —Tim Russert, *Wisdom of Our Fathers*

When I was researching the topic of fatherhood, I discovered an organization called the National Fatherhood Initiative (NFI). When I joined their organization, they sent me an NFI T-shirt, which had this on the back:

> Fathers, delivery room BE THERE, bath time BE THERE, first steps BE THERE, first day of school BE THERE, field trips BE THERE, birthday parties BE THERE, shooting hoops BE THERE, piano recitals BE THERE, driving test BE THERE, science projects BE THERE, first date BE THERE, swimming lessons BE THERE, high school graduation BE THERE, going away to college BE THERE, wedding day BE THERE, always BE THERE!

NFI's message is patently clear. The key to being an effective father is being involved with your children, thereby showing that you care. But "being there" is much more than just showing up. "Being there" is built on practicality and emotion.

DAD TIP:

There's the practical side of being a Dad, and there's the emotional side. Both are important. Both can be achieved by being there, both physically and mentally, for your child.

By practicality, I mean being involved in your child's physical safety, discipline, physical needs (such as helping with bathing and dressing when they are little), homework, car pools, and so on. By emotion, I mean listening, holding, sharing, teaching, caring, giving encouragement—all the things we need and deserve to lead full, healthy lives.

Being there goes beyond physical location. It means being intuitive—anticipating problems before they occur—and having the empathy and sympathy to understand what your children can't explain. Being there also means having the wisdom to see the connection between seemingly unrelated events and discovering new ways of defining or solving problems.

Lastly, being there means knowing when to establish new rules when new situations arise; for example, when a newborn comes home or when school begins. This sounds like a lot to ask, but the rewards make it all worthwhile, and it will happen naturally if you are just aware. Don't make it more difficult than it is; make it easy by being aware.

YOUR INFLUENCE IS IMMEASURABLE

> *"Children who can't find their fathers make one up or appropriate one to their liking, whether or not they call him 'Daddy.' In a young child who has not felt some form of masculine nurture, the hunger for a paternal presence can be insatiable."*
>
> —Kyle D. Pruett,
> "How Men and Children Affect Each Other's Development"

As a father, you are your child's hero, president, provider, king, protector, teacher, mentor, comforter, disciplinarian, and absolute connection to a successful future. Hopefully, you will also provide occasional comic relief.

As a man, you may feel the disappointments of life and struggle with the weaknesses we all have. But none of your failures matter to your child, and the only weakness that will harm your children is any weakness around seeing to their needs and well-being. Your greatest and lasting impact will be in your child's first three years. After that, you will continue to be an influence, but your leverage will decrease as they grow older. This decreasing level of influence is natural and healthy. But if your children have learned to trust you and respect you, your influence will always be there.

BEING THERE DOES NOT MEAN 24/7

I agree one hundred percent with the National Fatherhood Initiative about being there, but it's important to recognize that you'll be a more attentive Dad if you also take time for yourself. Beyond being fathers, we are many things—husbands, employees, friends, hobbyists, sports fans, artists, and individuals. If we feel we are slaves to our children, then we will develop a grudge, most likely subconscious, resulting in guilt and weaker relationships with our children. We need time to ourselves, for our business and other responsibilities.

"Being there" means as much as is practical and necessary, especially for the important events in your kids' lives, and being available when needed.

The key is to balance fathering and pursuing other needs and goals. You must be aware of conditions and situations that will take you away from your children, even if you are physically there. When you are too busy, or your mind is too occupied with nonessential worry or fretting, you will not be there for anyone.

START FATHERING WITH THEIR FIRST BREATH

If you were to plant a sapling oak tree and take care to water it, fertilize it, and properly trim it, this sapling would grow strong enough to withstand winds, ice storms, tire swings, and disease. But trees grown without attention are left to be shaped by nature itself. They may be littered with dead limbs and branches and lose their leaves early. Their roots may be shallow and their trunks hollow. Vines may smother them, or other trees may rob them of sunlight. Some of these neglected trees become misshapen by trying to grow under stressful situations or trying to survive between a rock and a hard place.

In these respects, children are no different from trees. Their chance to thrive is enhanced greatly by a father's (and a mother's) care, especially early care. Consider these examples:

- You can walk across the Mississippi near its source.
- Shrews defeated dinosaurs by eating their eggs.
- An architect can move an entire building before the foundation is poured.

A desired result has the greatest chance of occurring *when action is taken early*. Early recognition of a need and quick action to address that need have tremendous leverage. This truth also applies to fatherhood. There is no better time to start being there than at your child's birth. With newborns, communication doesn't come in the form of language. Your newborn senses your love through all five senses, but especially the feel of your touch, the sound of your voice, and the smiles they see on your face. These types of communication are key factors in forming a bond with your child.

Mothers have an advantage over fathers in that the baby has felt the vibrations of the mother's heart and voice for many months. The father's bonding must take place mostly after birth, and that bonding depends on the amount of contact you give the newborn. In fact, the first three years are when you will have the most impact on your child's life.

Babies need to be held, cuddled, and talked to. Allow your baby to lie quietly on your chest and feel the soothing beat of your heart and the gentleness of your breathing. Your deeper voice is a comfort to them, especially when they connect your voice to the safe feeling they have in your arms. Your smile is naturally interpreted by a newborn as a good, comforting, and loving act. If loved, held, and read to by you as a Dad in the first three years, your child develops a solid foundation in his or her relationship with you and is spared the psychological scars that so many young children experience when they don't receive the necessary love from their father. Because of this foundation, your children will be much more forgiving of any mistakes you make later in their lives.

In case it's not already intuitively obvious, neuroscientists performing brain research at Washington University in St. Louis have told my wife, who helped with their research through the Parents as Teachers organization, that there is a fertile "window of opportunity" during the early years of life when a child is most receptive to emotional, social, and intellectual stimulation (Maeroff). Without this stimulation, a child's development will suffer.

I will never forget a news report, years ago, by the ABC news program *20/20* about an orphanage in Romania where children were rarely held by human hands. They reacted to this lack of attention by rocking incessantly in their cribs, which were more like jail cells. These Romanian orphans received an estimated five to six minutes of attention a day.

According to Doctors Without Borders, "as a result of their troubled early lives, 1 in 10 of the children will finish life in a psychiatric institution, and all will suffer severe trauma." Eric Rosenthal of Disability Rights International said, "The eeriest thing about it was the near total silence. We heard one baby crying, and we asked about that baby. That baby had been placed the night before. But of the other children, we asked, 'Why aren't they crying?' And the staff said, 'We try our best, but we can't come to them when they cry.' So after a while they stop crying. They learn that there's no one there to take care of them."(Ahern and Rosenthal)

Thankfully, most children get much more attention than these Romanian orphans. This example magnifies the importance of human touch in children's early lives. It cannot be underestimated. Some is better than none. More is better than a little. Be there as the masculine touch they need so badly.

DAD TIP:

Never underestimate the value of loving human touch. Sometimes Dads think it's the Mom's job to hold, cuddle, and nurture their child. But this is wrong. Dads need to be involved, besides just being there, and give their young children the gift of loving human touch.

MISUNDERSTANDINGS ABOUT FATHERS AND INFANTS

Most people don't realize the impact fathers have on their infant children. Many men think young children don't really understand anything until they are older; then it's time for fathers to get more involved. But infants are actively engaged in unconscious learning long before understanding comes. They absorb things like a sponge. An infant's brain and nervous system without stimulation is like a sponge lying in the desert. In the wrong environment, the sponge is useless. There is nothing to soak up. The richness of the infant's mind needs nourishment, and the father is a source unique from the mother to provide this nourishment.

The evidence to support the importance of a father's love and attention is enormous. I could offer a lot of references, but you can search the Internet with a few key words and in very little time see the evidence for yourself. I just did a search after writing this and found the following quote in an article titled, "How Men and Children Affect Each Other's Development," by Kyle D. Pruett:

> If fathers have the capacity to nurture their children competently but differently from mothers, does this matter

to the children? Apparently so, according to two decades of research. Eight-week-old infants can discriminate between their fathers and their mothers, and respond in a differential way to their approach. Yogman compared videotapes of comfortably seated infants' response to their mothers' approach and their fathers'. In anticipation of their mothers picking them up, babies settled in, slowed their heart and respiratory rates, and partially closed their eyes. When they expected their fathers to hold them, babies hunched up their shoulders, widened their eyes, and accelerated their heart and respiratory rates.

Couples who adopt usually want to adopt infants. It's not just because this parallels the natural parenting process. When older children are adopted, they can have so many unknown or undiagnosed emotional and behavioral challenges. Most of these orphans did not have enough human touch or healthful interaction to develop normally. As warm, affectionate, and understanding as the new adoptive parents may be, they have a huge task before them to undo the harm of the child's early childhood experience.

Young children who live a few years without parents or a close equivalent do not absorb the love they need to develop normally. These unfortunate children were not given unconditional love and therefore think any love they get is conditional. This mindset sometimes takes a lifetime to get over.

BEING THERE FOR THE TEEN YEARS

Good parenting in the early years will significantly help you when your children become teens. Basic rules and mutual respect learned early on will go a long way. A child's adolescence, however, is a particularly tough time for a parent. Young teens and preteens are busy adjusting to their environment and find themselves in a sea of self-doubt, a maze of confusion, and the vise of constant peer pressure. Their mother and you, their father, may be considered the enemy, fighting against their wishes for freedom and justice.

In his book *Critical Connection: A Practical Guide To Parenting Young Teens*, Andy Kerckhoff, a father and middle school teacher, writes, "There are very few kids out there who will continue to defy an adult who takes the time to listen and communicate with them." Kerckhoff's book is a powerful resource in understanding and raising young teens. His guidance will help you understand what adolescents are going through and how to get through to them.

GENERATIONS CATCHING UP

Sometimes it takes a generation or two to make up for the lost link in the fatherhood chain. There are things I never taught my kids or thought to introduce them to. I didn't teach my young son how to swing a golf club or cast a fishing rod because I didn't know a thing about golf or fishing until I was in my forties. I never took my kids to a racetrack or a concert. I had never been to either so it didn't cross my mind. We never went camping as a family because I was never introduced to pitching a tent or using a Coleman stove.

DAD TIP:
If you didn't receive nurturing from your father, you may need to do some creative thinking about what activities you'd like to share with your child. We tend to do with our own children what our parents did with us when we were children. If that Dad link is missing in your past, start some new chapters and be creative in the activities you share with your own children.

Nothing whatsoever stopped me from doing these activities with my kids other than a complete lack of thought about them. I was not introduced to them as a kid. We just didn't do things with my dad. My interests came from activities I could do on my own, like following baseball.

I think back and see I could have been much more of a fun Dad, like my brother Bob is now. He takes his kids camping and to many other fun activities I never thought about.

Bob had the same father I did. Why does he do these things while I didn't? Bob had friends he clung to whose families *did* do these things. He had a surrogate family, so he learned about different activities than I did.

WHAT "*REALLY* BEING THERE" MEANS

Being around for your kids is the simplest yet most important part of being a father. You can do your own thing and at least be a masculine example. But *really* being there includes giving direction, showing your love for them, and providing the comfort they so often need. Fathering with love is the next step in the Pyramid of Dadhood. It's where we'll head in the next chapter.

YOUR ROAD MAP: CHAPTER 8

Start: Be there!

Major Highway: From infancy, your child understands your protective and loving touch, your gentle voice, the security of being with Dad. Don't squander your chance to make an impact, particularly in the first three years of your child's life. A Dad's presence is irreplaceable.

On the Open Road: If you didn't have a positive male influence as a child, think of what you wished for in a Dad. Then, be that person. Whether it means reading or playing outdoors with your child, taking your child with you when you shop for groceries, or holding your child when he or she is distressed, the greatest gift you can give your child is your presence.

Eighth Stop: Think about where you are regarding "being there." Are you physically present for your child? Are you mentally present? Do you balance this time with special time for you and your child's mother, as well as time for yourself? Being there for your child is positive and powerful. Do you have room to improve?

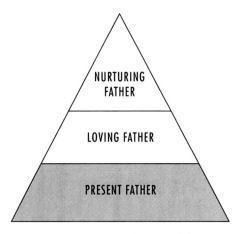

THE PYRAMID OF DADHOOD

CHAPTER 9

FATHERING WITH LOVE

"The need for love lies at the very foundation of human existence."

—The Dalai Lama

Love is living life without thought of reward. To be unaware of your own being while focusing on the welfare of someone else is true love. It is the warm blanket on a cold night, the net that catches you in a fall, the compass when you are hopelessly lost. This is the love children thrive on.

PROVIDE LOVE AND COMFORT

"Love is an irresistible desire to be irresistibly desired."

—Robert Frost

Robert Frost's quote is likely a tongue-in-cheek look at romantic love, but its equivalent for the father-child relationship could be "Love, to a child, is an irresistible need to be unconditionally wanted."

First, you must be there for your children. Once this is achieved, loving and comforting them may be the most important responsibilities and greatest gifts you can give. I've seen parents who set limits, protect their children, provide for their needs, insist on attention to schoolwork, teach respect and manners, and are there for them when they leave for school and when they get home. I don't downplay any of this and I praise it all, but these are just the mechanics of parenting. All the right actions are there, but real love and comforting are necessary, too, as the catalysts that make these acts successful.

Children need to feel your love through conversations, special moments together, and just knowing you will be there for their emotional needs. The difference between short-term foster parents and real parents (not necessarily birth parents) lies in the subtleties of *comfort* with safety and *love* with caring. Foster parents provide safety, but not the kind of comfort that comes from a child feeling settled in a family. Similarly, foster parents may be caring, providing for the needs of a child, but the highest need is parental love. When children experience safety with comfort and caring with love, they know they are important and valued, which lays a solid foundation for their growth.

Why is it so important to provide love with guardianship? Mihaly Csikszentmihalyi, a Hungarian psychology professor, wrote in his book *The Evolving Self*: "Children who feel unloved, or incompetent, or constantly guilty, or who feel manipulated or controlled by their parents, often will use up all their resources in an endless effort to prove that they are worthy of love and attention. Little energy is left over to wonder about the stars."

LET THEM KNOW YOU CARE

"If you want a slingshot, I hope your dad teaches you how to make one instead of buying one."
—Paul Harvey

You know what I wanted from my Dad? I wanted him to put his arm behind my back, grab my shoulder, and pull me into him—the kind of side-by-side hug Dads give. A simple act of caring can go a long way, and dads sometimes forget to do this, especially with their sons. Probably the most important thing your children need to learn from you is that you care. All children need a Dad to play with, to ask how they're doing, and to be ready to listen when they are excited, sad, or afraid. Not fulfilling such a basic need for your children can do immeasurable harm.

By giving your children your attention, they will have evidence of their self-worth. They will know someone cares for them besides Mom, and they will have someone to impress. We know that Moms and Dads often show caring in different ways. Generally, Moms soothe while Dads prepare. Moms protect and Dads challenge. Moms are often overlooked and taken for granted by their children, while Dads who interact tend to be more appreciated, especially when compared to less-involved dads. Make your relationship a standard for how a father-to-son or father-to-daughter relationship should be.

Caring, however, is not all comfort and attention. Caring is putting your foot down, too. Children need you to be their Dad, not just a friend. Hopefully, they will have plenty of others who will fulfill that role. Certainly you should be kind and warm, but you have responsibilities beyond friendship. Caring involves direction, correction, and measured discipline. Like taking foul-tasting medicine, your children may not like what you have to say at the time, but they will appreciate it later and be thankful. *All children want direction.*

GIVE YOUR KIDS THE FATHER THEY REALLY WANT

"Children need love, especially when they do not deserve it."
—Harold Hulbert

Kids don't always know it, but they want your love and your direction.

They want to know what the limits are. Young brains cannot judge danger because kids feel invincible. Children need to know the rules to succeed in society and need to have principles to base their decisions on. Having principles contributes to their self-esteem.

Children must learn that when no respect is given, no respect will be received; when no work is accomplished, no rewards will be forthcoming. When they fight you on the limits, dangers, rules, and principles you teach, don't interpret that as their desire for you to go away. They may think they want you to leave them alone, but if you did, they would be hurt deeply. Mostly, your kids need love and guidance, and you give them these gifts by being consistent and firm with them.

Too many times I have seen parents take the easy road and solve their children's problems for them. It's the easy way out for the parents because the issue goes away quicker and with less effort. What's worse, it's also the easy way out for the child because he or she is off the hook with little or no consequence and without learning life's lessons.

If you want your children to be stronger, you don't take them to the gym and lift the weights for them. If you want them to be smarter, you don't go to class for them and do their homework. Similarly, if you want them to learn the rules of life, you don't protect them from life. You must provide the way—give them a map and the rules of the road, but don't take the journey for them because they will not get anywhere that way. There must be consequences or there is no learning, and there must be boundaries to keep them on the right path.

DAD TIP:

What is fathering with love? It means, of course, being there, but it also involves helping your children make their own decisions, teaching them how to choose wisely, putting your foot down when they make poor decisions, and letting them know you love them, no matter what.

LISTEN

"The first duty of love is to listen."

—Paul Tillich

Sometimes all you have to do is listen. Children must know your love for them is real, even when they require discipline. You can't always fix things, although most Dads think this is what they must do. Often, just the ability to share fears or troubles with a loved one is all children need to do to purge their emotions. It is cathartic for them. They feel so much better by just being able to talk and to be listened to.

Get your children to talk. You learn more about your children from their questions than from their answers. With a question, your children are engaging you on their terms about a topic that is important to them. On the other hand, their answers to your questions can be less than honest to avoid a topic they are not ready to discuss. You have a crucial and high-impact responsibility as a father. Never stop listening, even when your children have children of their own.

ENCOURAGE

"It is easier to build strong children than to repair broken men."

—Frederick Douglass

A building with a strong foundation will withstand nature's wrath longer and need fewer repairs than will one with an unstable foundation. The same is true for children. To build children with a strong foundation, we need to love and encourage them early on.

Unsurprisingly, the word *encouragement* comes from the same word in French, meaning, "to give courage." So when you encourage someone, you are giving him or her courage to go on. Your encouragement will help your children face many challenges in life with confidence.

If your children's dreams are at risk, or they lose something important to them, then that is when your encouragement is needed most. The loss could be anything—a friend, a scholarship, a job, or not getting noticed or given credit for a significant accomplishment.

Teach them that when they lose something, there are ultimately only two things they can do: get it back, if possible, or let it go. While sounding like a simple concept, we all know it is not simple in practice, because making the decision to keep trying or to give up is not easy. Discussing this concept with your children will help them determine which path to take. Usually encouragement is associated with getting something back or continuing to try. But it also takes courage to let something go.

I've held on to and achieved most of my dreams. But I had to let go of the dream of being either a wide receiver or a third baseman—I just wasn't good enough as an athlete. Most of the dreams we might have to let go are those we have little or no control over. We cannot control what God-given potential we are born with, we cannot control other people, and we cannot control who our birth families are. We must teach our children that some circumstances must be accepted.

My wife was not enthusiastic about our son becoming an Army helicopter pilot because it is a dangerous occupation. But she knew what he wanted to do with his life and never discouraged him from that dream. So while she was unenthusiastic about that occupation for our son, she always supported him and his dreams. That is encouragement. That is love.

MINIMIZE PARENTAL PRESSURE

> *"Nothing has a stronger influence psychologically on their environment and especially on their children than the unlived life of the parent."*
>
> —C. J. Jung

I know a man who became a priest because he wanted to fulfill the dreams his parents had for him. They supported him all the way, encouraging him through his doubts about succeeding in this goal. Some would say they were excellent parents who worked hard to help their son become a respected man and a success. But this man never wanted to be a priest. He didn't know this for a while because his parents had drummed it into his head so much that he was convinced that he wanted this dream also.

Later, when he was in the seminary, this young man became aware, through observing the dedication of other seminarians and also the lives of his friends, of his lack of dedication and a feeling of being unfulfilled. He didn't feel right about the priesthood, because it wasn't *his* chosen vocation. Through the pressure of his parents and the momentum of a life devoid of free will, he became a priest.

Knowing and supporting your children's dreams should be an unselfish endeavor. Don't discourage them from learning about those things they are most interested in. Their natural interest is often the fuel that will take them to success in that topic or field. We fathers dream of sharing our interests with our sons and daughters. It is natural, and I encourage you to do so, but don't push them into your interests. It is their life to live, not yours. Of course, introduce them to your interests—that's part of being a Dad.

Two of my big passions are baseball and flying. As a Dad, I certainly dreamed about my son becoming a great baseball player or a pilot. As it turns out, he has an interest in those activities too. He was introduced to them through my interest, but I never pushed him to either.

DAD TIP:

Think of pressures others have put upon you, perhaps making you go in directions you would not have chosen for yourself. As you mold your children, remember to shape them into the people they naturally want to be; do not force them to forgo their dreams to meet yours.

BE AWARE

"You can observe a lot just by watching."

—Yogi Berra

There's probably nothing more satisfying to parents than to see their children succeed, and knowing your love and support helped them achieve their success makes it all the better. Life sometimes gets in the way, however, and we may become unaware of our children's accomplishments and anxieties. We can't let our everyday challenges and duties mask us from our children's lives. Being there is important, but being *aware* is a highly important subset.

By "being aware," I mean knowing when your children need encouragement or support, when they need a pat on the back or a kick in the rear (not a literal kick!). Both pats on the back and kicks in the rear provide positive momentum if your children are heading the right way.

Seemingly little things that upset our kids may get past us. They may be failing at something important to them. It's not likely they will volunteer that information, and we may not notice when they need our encouragement. You must then listen, be interested, ask nonthreatening questions, and find a connection with them. You most likely had a similar time of discomfort, trouble, or sadness. With older children, it's best not to tell them what to do but to suggest things to think about. It is also important to be yourself when you speak to your kids. If you read a book such as this one and try to give book answers, they will see right through you. You must translate what you learn into your own style and language.

ENCOURAGE PASSION AND BEWARE OF ADDICTION

"Your reason and your passion are the rudder and the sails of your seafaring soul."

—Kahlil Gibran, *The Prophet*

If asked what I would want for my children beyond health and happiness, I would answer "passion." Passion is an elusive quality and should not be wasted. More lasting than enthusiasm and deeper than mere interest, passion is inspiration with momentum. Sometimes its origin is unexplainable, but passion is an inexpensive and efficient fuel, like wind in the sails, providing impetus toward focused goals.

Recall the passions of your life to your children and share the excitement you felt at those times. As a parent, you can't provide passion, but you can influence and support it. Let's say your daughter loves animals. She can't resist any interaction with horses, dogs, or even ferrets. You may not be interested in animals yourself, but that is not important. What is important is your child's passion that may become a lifelong occupation or hobby.

Another wonderful aspect of passion is how it keeps us in the present. When in the present, your children are not fretting over the past, nor are they afraid of the future. They are pleasantly lost in the timeless now, and when that happens, you see them in their truest state of happiness.

Suppose your son is discouraged about a failure. Maybe he doesn't make his high school baseball team. His continued passion can help him overcome that failure by working hard to make next year's team, or that failure may help him acquire a passion for something else more suited for him. Maybe football or golf will take over his competitive nature. Either way, moving forward is key. Passionate children are usually happy children. Passionate people are usually enthusiastic about sharing their love and knowledge of a subject, creating friendships and fostering communication skills. Any shyness someone may have takes a backseat to sharing his or her passion.

However, when passion takes your child away from normal relationships or development, you need to step in. Passion is a great fuel as long as it is taking your son or daughter to a good place. But an obsessive passion is harmful to a balanced lifestyle. While passion is mostly good, some types of passion are not. Video games can be a passion, but when that passion robs someone of personal relationships, sleep, or exercise, then it is quite harmful. Food can be a passion, but it can also be an addiction. A passion becomes an addiction when you can't control it. While a passion provides energy, an addiction robs you of energy. Knowing when a passion is becoming an addiction can be a tough call for parents. One hint: a passion will take your child to a good place, while an addiction will certainly take your child to a bad one.

In *Fables of Aesop and Other Eminent Mythologists*, translated by Roger L'Estrange, we have this moral: "It is with our passions as it is with fire and water; they are good servants, but bad masters."

REMEMBER THE PLIABILITY OF YOUTH

"However far the stream flows, it never forgets its source."
—Nigerian proverb

I repeat an earlier plea to start fathering immediately with this instructive analogy: Potters start with soft clay, shaping it into bowls, pots, vases, and other beautiful works of art using their hands or intricate molds. When the clay is soft, any impression an artisan desires is possible. But after the clay has hardened, it will be almost impossible to change. Later attempts to change the shape can only be artificial and may destroy the piece. Pottery can be filled with oil, water, and even earth, but they all can be easily poured out because the contents are not part of the pottery. Similarly, children can try new things and be influenced by others, but the values you have molded will remain. Soft clay left untouched by the artisan will harden to the shape it was left in, rarely as beautiful as something the potter shaped, not as admired nor as useful, and likely ignored.

Your infant children are also soft clay, hardening gradually month by month, and you are the artisan, making them beautiful and useful. Their beauty is exhibited by the way they carry themselves and the joy they bring to others. Their usefulness is manifested when they become confident and self-reliant contributors to society. You must not wait to mold your children. The longer you wait, the less impact you will have on them and their future. Remember, your influence decreases each year as they cure into their own shape.

Certainly, each child is born with his or her own characteristics just as each type of clay has different, unchangeable traits. But every child and every type of clay can be molded significantly. Once you have grasped the significance of your early involvement as a father, the next question you must ask yourself is this: "What skills do I have as the artisan helping to shape my children's lives?" After all, some potters are better than others. Well, there is good news for you. The most basic skills necessary to be a good influence as a father are love and attention. You will find that you have the talent already if you just place your hands upon the clay.

PREVENTION IS EASIER THAN HEALING

This book is more about prevention than healing. That is why your attention as a father must start immediately. When maladjusted children are identified early on, smaller remedies can cure what may be incurable if left unchecked.

> **DAD TIP:**
> *This book is more about prevention than healing. That is why your attention as a father should start immediately.*

Your children will do whatever works to get your attention. If you let their misbehavior control you, be prepared to see that type of behavior often, unless you begin to show them it won't work any longer. Young children are ingenious—getting attention is a skill they come by naturally. They may have tried something on you and saw that it worked. Or they may have witnessed an attention-getting technique of other children and saw that it got them what they wanted.

Of course, they will test you. Let them know unequivocally that bad behavior will not be tolerated or condoned. Paramount in this is being consistent as a parent; without consistency on your part, they will not respect your authority.

BE AS CONSISTENT AND RELIABLE AS THE SUNRISE

Nothing ruins a child's respect for a parent like a promise or a punishment unfulfilled. It cannot be repeated often enough: without consistency there is no order, just chaos. Within your family, inconsistency will confuse your children and cause you to lose whatever respect you may have gained. They will ignore your idle threats. They will doubt your promises. Their memory of you will be clouded. And they will see you as a shell and not a rock.

Adhering to consistent rules and an unshakable philosophy can be challenging. But it is easier if you do these three things:

- Have an idea, plan, or approach to parenting you can believe in.
- Be aware of what you are doing when you are doing it—in other words, are you following your plan?
- Have basic values you always live by, such as:
  » Respect for others
  » Honesty and integrity in all you do
  » Doing what is best and not what is easiest

Having an idea of what you are doing and why is a simple and obviously intelligent approach to consistent parenting. But too often emotions, traditions, or habits override the plan. If you have rules for your children, believe in those rules and be able to explain them. Be conscious of your parenting plan and all you do and say. This will help keep you from being unreasonable and will firmly establish a habit of speaking and acting in a way that supports your plan.

DAD TIP:

I cannot say this enough: Consistency is vital for your children. You must be consistent in your love, in your expectations, in your presence, and in your rules. No child can thrive in a wishy-washy environment, where the rules are ever-changing and your attentiveness is sporadic.

Here are some essential values to consider: Cultivating a habit of *respect* will ensure you treat everyone respectfully. Being *honest* will not place undue pressure on your memory. Having *integrity* will gain others' trust. *Doing what is best* and not what is easiest will sometimes take guts and extra work on your part. (For example, giving in to your screaming child in public is easier, but not what is best to prevent a recurrence.) And it is hard work—consistent and respected fathers remember what they say and do, keep their promises, and are rarely lazy.

KNOW THE POWER OF HABITS

Advice is something we all can use but rarely regard. It's not that we don't want to; we just forget about it or quit too easily. I can tell my nephew to save some of his earnings, that it will serve him well in the future, and he will likely agree. But I would be happily shocked if he followed through. I know physical exercise would be good for me, and every day I plan on starting again. I may even run a couple of days in a row, but I won't keep it up. Why? Because what comes most easily to us are those actions or activities that are habits, whether good or bad. Exercise won't become a real part of my life until I make it a habit. Bad habits have tremendous power over our lives, but I want to concentrate only on developing good habits here, especially since good habits often overcome bad habits.

Children are susceptible to forming habits. You see this when they are babies and toddlers. Change their routine and they will let you know about it. When you've established a time to eat, they want to eat. When it's their bedtime, they need to sleep. We can take advantage of the law of habit to teach our children good habits.

Some habits we should ingrain in our children at the earliest opportunity are:

- Politeness
- Sharing
- Saving (enjoying good things over time, rather than seeking instant gratification)

You can recommend an action to others that can change their life, but it will not take hold unless it is ingrained through repetition and then acted on regularly. It takes time, patience, and attention, but teaching your children politeness and sharing will disarm those your kids come into contact with, creating a favorable atmosphere for them. Saving will teach them the self-reliance and self-discipline they will need to be successful and happy.

BREAK FROM ROUTINE TO CREATE MEMORIES

"May you live all the days of your life."
—Jonathan Swift

Routines beget habits, consistency, comfort, and discipline. They are a safe place to return to but are not good to stay in constantly or forever. Routine for older children can be a bore and not conducive for growth, so breaks from routine can be good, fun, and also quite simple.

A favorite memory of mine is when my father took me in his truck to haul sod one day. It was so cool to be with him alone and to ride in that huge, loud, smoke-billowing truck while he shifted gears like he was deftly handling a baton. I can visualize it clearly to this day. It was a simple but wonderful change from my monotonous days.

You rarely remember moments performed in a routine. You may remember the routine, but seldom a particular moment. But you will remember a time when the routine is broken, such as making a special breakfast before school instead of instant oatmeal, or turning off the TV one evening to play family board games, or letting your kids stay up late, even on a school night, to see a predicted asteroid shower.

You and your children will remember these special moments fondly, even more fondly as the years go by. I vividly remember stopping in the middle of an Illinois cornfield to show our kids the Milky Way galaxy in the darkness, far away from any city. I wish I had been aware enough to do these spontaneous activities more often as a father.

Here is a note from my younger daughter, Rachel, thanking me for a simple surprise when she was in high school.

> Hey Dad,
>
> Remember that night over 5 years ago when I walked in the house after a shift at Gordman's? It was about 10 p.m., all the lights were off, and all of a sudden "Jacob's Ladder" came on—BLARING! It was so weird. I couldn't figure out where it came from—and how anyone knew it was my favorite song at the time. You being all tricky with the fancy Bose remote from up in bed. I remember being all freaked out at the time, but then so excited to have that song! That was fun—thanks for that.
>
> Love, Rachel

I think she will remember that little surprise from the stereo forever, as I will always cherish her note.

CREATE FAMILY TRADITIONS

Family traditions create great memories. Simple examples are going to Grandma's every Sunday for dinner or getting ice cream at your favorite spot on summer weekends. In St. Louis, it was at Ted Drewes Frozen Custard where we and hundreds of others spent warm summer evenings. At my wife's insistence, we also picked apples in the fall at Eckert's Orchard across the river in Illinois, and I'm happy we did. The memories of your family traditions will remind your children how much fun they had as kids. You just need to be creative.

Rachel sent me another note regarding one of our family traditions. I had recently asked her to go to a St. Louis Cardinals baseball game with me, and she was excited to go. Before the date of the game, she sent me this note inside a sweet card that told me she felt "really lucky" that I was her Dad. The note read:

> I remember . . . Cardinal games at Busch Stadium with you when I was a little girl . . . Mom would put my hair up in a ponytail with my red and white Cardinal bow.
>
> At the beginning of the game we would plan our nacho trip for the 3rd or 4th inning . . . Other than the nachos, I was most excited for the hat dance and the 7th inning stretch.
>
> You would explain the top of the inning vs. the bottom (which was which). And explain to me why the people were excited or sad. And assure me that the losers would be all right.
>
> I was always nervous to go to the bathroom without you so you would watch me in line and wait right outside for me.
>
> At the end of the game we would shuffle through the crowds stepping on old cups and trash. You would lead me with your hand as I was towered by other people—feeling like I was in a hole.
>
> And of course I would complain about listening to more coverage (on the radio) on the way home.
>
> Thanks for that.
>
> I love you,
>
> Rachel

You might not necessarily get notes of thanks and appreciation from your kids, but know that they love what you do for them. Traditions will bring your family together to create a special bond that will stand the test of time.

YOUR ROAD MAP: CHAPTER 9

Start: Consider what it means to you to "father with love."

Major Highway: Remember that one of the roads to your children's hearts is to be attentive to them. Staying attentive and involved throughout your children's lives will create wonderful relationships with them as time goes on. Listen to them when they are happily chattering or when they are trying to work through difficulties. Create family traditions that can potentially maximize these listening opportunities, with surprises built in along the way.

On the Open Road: Imagine new ways to father with love. It does not necessarily take money or lots of time to break out of the routine and do something unexpectedly fun with your child.

Ninth Stop: What good experiences have you had as a present father? What can you do to be even better at offering your love and comfort to your children?

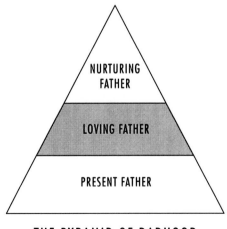

THE PYRAMID OF DADHOOD

CHAPTER 10

BUILDING STRONG CHILDREN

"We cannot always build the future for our youth, but we can build our youth for the future."

—Franklin D. Roosevelt

We can be fairly good fathers by doing very little: being present and being engaged. But we can be *great* fathers, true Dads, through teaching, coaching, and mentoring. Being there for our children and loving them may be more important, but building strong children takes the most effort.

THE LEVERAGE OF LOVE AND CHARACTER

"Give me a lever long enough, and a place on which to rest it, and I will move the world."

—Archimedes

We should all understand the influence of leverage. Leverage provides power without the need for significant force. As you lose leverage, your power to influence ultimately becomes dependent on force alone. Force without leverage often comes in the form of dominance or even violence, and in the end it is not nearly as powerful as good leverage. Mahatma Gandhi influenced others with the leverage of his insight and character, while Saddam Hussein influenced others with the force of threats and violence. Leverage works in the domain of respect, whereas force works in the domain of fear.

Love may be the most perfect "lever" ever devised! With love, your influence will require virtually no force at all. As a father, *your greatest leverage is when your children are young.* It is then that you establish your influence. You can't *force* anyone to change—not really. But you can *influence* people to change by teaching, mentoring, and being a good example or model. However, simply having influence or leverage is not enough, because leverage is a tool without a conscience. Influence can be used either for good or evil, because while you may gain a type of respect through influence, it doesn't necessarily follow that your influence will be beneficial.

Force can be frightening for our young ones, but respect can also misguide them. Think of cult leaders who lead through the leverage of cultivated respect, but who realistically can be as dangerous as axe-wielding psychopaths.

Character is the key here. A father must have good character to use his influence properly. Having good character and knowing how to influence others, using respect and being respectful, you will have all the tools necessary to be an outstanding Dad. Always remember: the power of leverage is so much more effective than the power of force.

If fathers use the leverage of love and character, adhering to the basic principles of fatherhood noted in the Pyramid of Dadhood, they will certainly influence the lives of their children in a positive and most satisfying way. If a young father is mentored properly, he will use these principles. But without any guidance, without any knowledge of these principles, a young father can feel an enormous burden. A young man whose father abandoned him will often inherit this burdened feeling in his role as a father.

DAD TIP:

Did you ever learn about "simple tools" as a kid? I learned about pulleys, levers, wedges, screws, wheels, axles, and inclined planes as simple tools that let me do more with little force. The concept of one simple machine, the lever, applies best to parenting and the influence you have with your children. Force and might can win, but at what cost? Using the leverage of love helps your children grow in a world of safety instead of fear.

As done here, using the metaphor of a lever, sometimes it helps as a father to approach a problem using examples that are more familiar to you and your children.

LIKE FATHER, LIKE SON (OR DAUGHTER)

> *"Don't worry that your children never listen to you. Worry that they are always watching you."*
> —Robert Fulghum

One thing you need not worry about—it will happen with certainty—is this: your children *will* learn from you. They learn in two ways: First, they learn by what you point out to them that they may never see on their own. I call this parenting. Second, they observe and mimic you. I call this as parental osmosis.

In parental osmosis, your influence can take two opposite paths. One is as a good example in which your children want to emulate your kindness or wisdom. The other is as a terrible example in which they will try their best *not* to be the uncaring, slothful, or cruel parent they have seen exemplified by you. The worst outcome of all is when your children assume that your bad behavior is the correct behavior, and so that is what they emulate. To be the best influence, you must be a person of clear character and integrity, not only in their eyes, but in truth, in life, and in all things.

Take stock of your values and actions. If you are rude to your elders, your children will most likely be rude to theirs. If you smile often, they are more likely to smile than not. If you smoke, they will see that as an endorsement for smoking, even if you tell them not to. If you always do what you say you will do, they will learn to do the same.

DAD TIP:

Our children learn from us in two ways. They learn by what you point out to them that they may never see on their own. And they learn by watching us. How we act matters just as much as what we intentionally teach.

Notwithstanding ADHD, bipolar, and other disorders, when your children do have behavioral issues, it may have more to do with you than you may think or admit. Often the habits, traits, and misdeeds of your children are just magnifications of your own values and actions. A mother who gossips is more likely to have a daughter who gossips. A selfish, self-centered father may have a son or daughter who, if mishandled, can be even more selfish and self-centered.

You will see parental osmosis in friends, neighbors, and your own family if you look closely enough. To teach your children well, you must know yourself well. I wonder how many people even see their own flaws. It's quite common to hear people criticize others for flaws they themselves have. The flaw is so close to them that they easily recognize it in others and are quick to criticize, but without objective introspection they can't see it in themselves. Most parents will never link their children's flaws to their own, and few will see their children's learned flaws as serious, if they see them at all. But your positive choices and actions also flow to your children.

When he was in third grade, our son had a classmate that he described as a "city kid," which meant he was bused in from the city. We didn't think much of this description until we realized this "city kid" was African-American. His view of this boy was through his own experience, not based on the prejudices of others—our son never regarded this boy as different in ways of race or color, only in how he got to school. At this point in his life, he seemingly had not been influenced by racial bias. As his parents, my wife and I take partial credit for this.

Robert Coles states in *The Moral Intelligence of Children*, "The most persuasive moral teaching we adults do is by example: the witness of our lives, our ways of being with others and speaking to them and getting on with them—all of that is taken in slowly, cumulatively, by our sons and daughters, our students." And further, "In the long run of a child's life, the unself-conscious moments that are what we think of simply as the unfolding events of the day and the week turn out to be the really powerful and persuasive times, morally."

SELF-REFLECTION

> "When I do good, I feel good; when I do bad, I feel bad. That's my religion."
>
> —Abraham Lincoln

While your children will watch you without hesitation, tell them to "watch themselves" also, to observe what they themselves are doing and determine why they are doing it. Too often, young people react without understanding their motives and actions. Without reflection, they end up making wrong choices, getting into trouble, saying the wrong things, and not learning from mistakes. If they know how to reflect on their actions, reactions, and decision-making processes, it will help them cope the next time they face a similar situation.

Reflecting on their actions and reactions also helps children mature much faster. Only a mature child will think and act this way. Try it yourself, and then teach your kids how to do it. It will benefit them to learn and practice self-reflection.

DAD TIP:

Our kids watch us and learn from us from the earliest ages, even infancy. Be the man you want your children to model. As they get older, help them see what their actions tell others, and that life is all about the choices they make. They need to know why they make the choices they do, and how these choices impact both their own lives and those of others.

PEER PRESSURE TESTS INTEGRITY

"If it is not right, do not do it; if it is not true, do not say it."

—Marcus Aurelius

Your children should understand that when they have emotions, those emotions are telling them something, and they shouldn't be ignored. A bad feeling in your gut or tightness in your throat is not something you consciously bring about. Depending on age and emotional maturity, any person can learn right from wrong from the messages their body is sending.

When I was a young teen, I was hanging out with some friends of a friend of mine. It turned out they had a different set of values than I had. That night, with me as a passenger, they drove around and turned over people's trash cans in a local neighborhood. I wasn't happy about this at all, but had little influence (or the guts) to stop them. Besides, I thought I would look like a sissy to them for not going along: classic peer pressure.

I remember a sick feeling in the pit of my stomach as this was happening. It wasn't from being afraid of getting caught; it was because it was so wrong, so stupid and immature. That feeling in my stomach told me

I didn't want to be like them, and I never had anything to do with them again.

They had somehow become desensitized to the difference between right and wrong, and I didn't allow myself to spend time with them and become desensitized myself. They seemingly accepted this group behavior individually, or maybe not. Peer pressure is a tough thing to deal with when you are young. It takes courage, strength, and integrity to stand apart. Your children need to know they have the support of their parents when taking a stand. They need your advice, and you should always be open with them. Otherwise, the advice they seek and follow will come from other sources.

I once stole a candy bar just to see if it was possible. I was successful in my thievery, but when I got home, I took one bite and threw the rest away. My remorse was telling me I had done something wrong. I could not enjoy an act that was not in keeping with the person I really was deep inside.

But not all children are the same. Some do not have the same values or remorse to help keep them straight. These children can more easily fall prey to peer pressure. If your child tends not to be remorseful for unethical acts, your parenting skills will be tested and you may need professional help.

CHARACTER FLAWS

Character flaws include things like rudeness, lying, and bullying. When flaws in character exist, they have to do with the values these children live by. Children will rarely decide to be rude or dishonest when they've been taught proper values.

However, I don't suggest you teach your children to be pushovers. They need to be taught to stand up for whatever they believe in. But being firm does not imply being rude, and that lesson also pertains to parents. You can politely correct, you can firmly hold on to your beliefs without offending others, and you can graciously and respectfully disagree with a position or argument.

Of course, sometimes we can be rude for no other reason than we are upset. As a father, you might be rude to your children by ignoring them at the wrong time, by overpunishing them, by letting anger rule you, by treating them as unimportant, by interrupting them, and so much more. When you catch yourself being rude, especially in front of or to your kids, correct yourself and apologize, if appropriate—and usually it is appropriate, even if difficult.

ETHICAL BEHAVIOR

"Character is higher than intelligence."
—Ralph Waldo Emerson

Consider how your children reach their decisions. Do they make decisions through fear of reprisal or through integrity? For example, suppose you were to ask them if they would ever steal a candy bar from a store. They would surely say no. Then ask them why. If they say they would be afraid they might get caught, then you have a decision made through fear (and a possible problem with values). If they answer that stealing is wrong, then that is an ethical decision made through integrity.

How many young people do you know who understand ethics or even know what it means? In math courses, we're taught methodologies to answer problems that involve multiplication, division, addition, and subtraction. In English, we're taught sentence structure. In science, we're taught theories and formulas. But when we teach our kids right from wrong, it is usually in the form of "Don't do this, and don't do that." It becomes a memory game, and sometimes parents do not consistently apply the dos and don'ts, causing the child much confusion. Ethics is a moral philosophy you impart to your child through teaching or example. When you say, "Do this," or "Don't do that," it is the equivalent of giving your children fish. But when you pass on a moral philosophy like the Golden Rule, it is the equivalent of teaching them to fish.

SELF-RELIANCE

"If you want children to keep their feet on the ground, put some responsibility on their shoulders."

—Abigail Van Buren

Self-reliance is a quality any person must have to survive and succeed. Imparting it to children requires parents to be proactive. A father can take special interest in teaching this quality to his children by observing what a busy mother might not.

Life is a gift, but one must unwrap the present to enjoy it. Similarly, a child must struggle with problems and overcome obstacles to learn. Strength comes in the form of confidence when a child succeeds, and in the form of experience, learning, and determination when a child does not succeed. One of the first examples of overcoming failure is when a baby is learning to walk. Without some expected falls, the young child would never master walking.

DAD TIP:
Some key areas where the power of Dadhood is truly revealed include helping your children achieve self-reliance, build self-confidence, use and enjoy their imagination for life, and learn to set, plan for, and achieve age-appropriate goals. All will serve them well as they mature into adulthood.

Failure will teach children where they need to improve. Weak people blame their failures on others and, therefore, they assume they have nothing to learn. The first step to growth is to accept responsibility. The next step is to make corrections, on your own if possible.

Getting help is a human need and expectation, but not always the best way to become self-reliant. Asking for help can be an admission of not having control, which is all right for a two-year-old, but not a twenty-two-year-old. Start teaching the *attitude* of self-reliance as soon as possible. Teach your children to tie their own shoes, button their own sweater, and do their own homework. This early training will encourage them to have an independent nature. Be a teacher of independence, not an enabler of the easy way out.

My daughter Rachel kept a diary when she was an adolescent. A few months ago, she was reading it and came to me laughing. She found a passage she wrote when she was worried, nervous, and upset about a test she was going to take the next day at school. Rachel had kept coming to me and her mom asking us if we thought she would pass. Our response was to tell her to study and do the best she could. That evening, she came into our room and asked that we pray for her to pass this "monumental" test. In her diary she quoted me, and even with my bad memory I remember my answer: "You take care of your test! I'll pray you are responsible." Passing the test was her responsibility; how well she did depended on her efforts. She passed the test easily.

> **DAD TIP:**
> *When you help your children cope with and instinctively enjoy their lives, then you rarely need to comfort them due to their enhanced maturity. They welcome your encouragement out of trust, your suffering through their errors is reduced, and your need to punish them becomes rare.*

IT ALL DEPENDS ON *YOU*

> *"Believe in your strength and your youth. Learn to repeat endlessly to yourself, 'It all depends on me.'"*
>
> —André Gide

This quote by André Gide struck me, especially the suggestion to repeat to yourself, "It all depends on me." Teach this quote to your child when he or she is old enough to understand it, and if the lesson sinks in, you've made a quantum leap in preparing your child for life. A child taught self-reliance when young will understand more quickly that it *always* depends on oneself—to listen, to learn, to act, to take responsibility, to fight fear, to pray for guidance, to ignore doubters, to take the bull by the horns.

Paradoxically, those young people who have this attitude are the ones that get the most help and best advice. People love to help those who show the gumption to help themselves, and they love winners and want to be in their corner. But they give up on those who won't help themselves. Capable but dependent people are weaklings, usually dependent on their friends and family or on welfare from strangers. They became dependent by leaning on those who cater to their weaknesses, and therefore they stay in the "poor me" cesspool.

If your daughter learns that her success depends on her own decisions and actions, she will want to learn the skills and attitudes that will lead to success. The attitude of "it all depends on me" is the powerful lens that will bring focus to your children's lives. This attitude alone does not define success, but allows it. This is a life-changing attitude, and when young people grasp its power, their lives take off.

The first thought that may come into a child's head when they hear "it all depends on you" is fear. That's a startling revelation for kids. It puts pressure on them to perform. The puppet strings have been cut and they must stand on their own. But in place of the puppet strings is a stage with a producer (Mom), a director (Dad), and a supporting cast (family). How effective a director can you be?

ENCOURAGE IMAGINATION

"The moment you doubt whether you can fly, you cease for ever to be able to do it."

—J. M. Barrie, *Peter Pan*

A father once found his four-year-old daughter typing on his computer keyboard. He asked her what she was doing, and she replied, "I'm writing a story." He then asked her what the story was about, and she said, "I don't know, Daddy. I can't read." This little girl had quite an imagination. She knew she was putting out a story, and it didn't matter what it was about. Simply taking a joy ride on Daddy's computer, she didn't have a plan, nor did she need one. That would come later. When children are imagining, they are learning to fly, and practice makes perfect. Later on, their imagination skills can be refined to include flight planning and dreaming up places to go and things to be. Dads can encourage their children's imagination by reading bedtime stories, playing make-believe, or just leaving them creative tools to play with on their own. Don't be afraid if they have imaginary friends or talk to stuffed animals. Communication skills need practice, too.

Supporting our children's dreams includes staying out of the way of those dreams, or better yet, encouraging their creativity. In his book *Creativity: Flow and the Psychology of Discovery and Invention*, Mihaly Csikszentmihalyi interviews many of the most creative people on Earth.

What he found out about their families is fascinating. Only about ten percent of these creative geniuses are from middle-class families. Most are from families of intellectuals where creative pursuits were strongly encouraged, while about thirty percent are from poor but hard-working families. The secret to creative success seems to be encouragement to pursue intellectual activity, either by those parents who know its value firsthand, by those parents who know its potential in making the lives of their children better, or by their children who recognize its potential. At ten percent, the middle class falls last. Maybe they're too comfortable to dream and not particularly pushed toward intellectual pursuits—that's not an environment that stimulates creativity. No matter where you find yourself on the economic or intellectual ladder, keep in mind your role in your children's creativity.

GOALS AND THE BOY WHO WANTED TO BE A FIREFIGHTER

My friend Dale once told me the story of his son Mike, who knew at a young age exactly what he wanted to do with his life. Before discussing Mike's story, I want to mention four simple steps to achieving goals. If you complete all these steps, you will likely achieve any goal you set.

1. Know yourself well. Know and accept your desires and capabilities.
2. Decide clearly and honestly where you want to go.
3. Develop a plan to get there.
4. Have the right attitude to keep your plan in action.

When Mike was twelve, Dale took him to the local firehouse to join the Explorers, which Dale described as "a kind of Boy Scouts with hoses." When they got there, the Captain told them Mike had to be fourteen before he could join. Mike was disappointed, but there was nothing he could do except wait.

On his fourteenth birthday, Mike went to Dale again and said, "Let's go to the firehouse, Dad." Dale had forgotten his son's desire to join the Explorers but was happy to take him there. When they got to the firehouse this time, the Captain told Mike the program had ended because there was not enough interest. Again Mike was disappointed but not discouraged. The next day, he started to recruit his friends and others to join him in starting a new Explorers program. Before long, Mike had his group of friends all wanting to be Explorers. The program was successful and the fire chief even got an award for starting up the new Explorer post.

Mike had a clear interest and goal that drove him every day. With Mike's focus and the support of his parents all along, there was no way he would not reach his goal. In my mind, Dale's son, Mike, is one of the most successful people anywhere. He may not make a lot of money, and not many would want his job, but some millionaires are not doing what they really want to do in life. Mike is doing exactly what he wants to do, and it's one of the most honorable professions. Today, Mike is chief of the Liberty Fire Department in Missouri.

Mike had an inherent passion that automatically took care of steps one and two: know yourself, and know where you want to go. Step three, planning, had begun but still needed attention. However, step four, having the right attitude, is easy when you have a strong desire. As a parent, you are fortunate if your child has a passion. Most kids don't know what they want to do with their lives, but when they are ready, you can help them figure it out based on their skills and interests and remind them of the four steps to achievement.

DAD TIP:

The Four Steps of Attaining a Goal

1. *Know yourself well. Know and accept your desires and capabilities.*
2. *Decide clearly and honestly where you want to go.*
3. *Develop a plan to get there.*
4. *Have the right attitude to keep your plan in action.*

EDUCATION IS CRUCIAL

"Perhaps the most valuable result of all education is the ability to make yourself do the thing you have to do, when it ought to be done, whether you like it or not; it is the first lesson that ought to be learned; and however early a man's training begins, it is probably the last lesson that he learns thoroughly."
—Thomas H. Huxley

"When the student is ready, the teacher will appear."
—Proverb

These quotes are true whether your child is three or thirty. When it comes to some things you want your children to learn, like walking, potty training, or riding a bike, you just have to wait until they are ready.

Occasionally, there is a clash between the truth of this philosophy and the practicality of the situation.

If your child isn't interested in school, it's not likely he or she will do well. You can take your children to school, but you can't make them learn. It can be a battle because you just can't let them fall behind.

As in many things, early preventive measures are better than searching for a cure later on. The preventive measures in this case involve opening your children's eyes early on to adventures and wonders, such as a trip to the zoo, reading to them regularly, or vacations to interesting places. These will open their horizons and stimulate their natural curiosities.

Early experiences and an environment of learning have a great impact on the brain of a child. Canyons carved by rivers first took shape from the paths of raindrops that fell millions of years ago. The networks of the brain act in a similar way. Early impressions will be marked deeply into the neural networks of a child's brain. Experiences can cause a path to pleasure or a path to pain. The next stimulation will take the paths of least resistance in the brain.

Too much negative stimulation will cause a path that always leads to pain, and then that path will be blocked to avoid the pain. Positive stimulation will lead to pleasure and a desire to continue. Your goal as a Dad is to create an environment of learning that is fun and positively stimulating and that leads to a craving for knowledge, exploration, and discovery.

> *"Just as eating against one's will is injurious to health, so studying without a liking for it spoils the memory, and it retains nothing it takes in."*
>
> —Leonardo da Vinci

Teaching your children *how* to think as opposed to *what* to think is a priceless gift they can use forever in their education and life in general. Just as it is more important to teach a man to fish than to give him a fish, a child with the ability to think can face the world with more courage and less vulnerability.

From the youngest ages, challenge them often with riddles or simple questions. Get them to a place where they enjoy solving puzzles. Help them learn how to find answers and where to go to learn more about something that fascinates them.

You are hurting your children's problem-solving skills when you do their homework for them. Certainly you should help them understand principles and lessons, but they must prove they can solve or analyze problems on their own. What good is it if they get an A on "your" homework? They learn nothing, and it sends them all the wrong signals.

THE DRY-SPONGE ANALOGY

"Children have to be educated, but they have also to be left to educate themselves."

—Ernest Dimnet

"Too often we give children answers to remember rather than problems to solve."

—Roger Lewin

"Why?" children ask. "Why do I have to study [fill in the blank with literature, math, science, basket weaving 404, or any other subject] if I never plan to use it?"

Well, there's a good reason. Your infant children are like dry sponges, soaking up everything around them. Hearing words and sounds, sensing emotions, seeing images, touching objects—all experiences are rich and enriching. As they get older, their learning sponge becomes more and more saturated, unable to absorb as much as before. The only way we can get their sponge to continue soaking up more knowledge is to make the sponge bigger. Education does this for them.

Students may not totally understand what they are learning right away, but the new lessons expand their minds, making their sponge bigger, allowing them to absorb more and to pick up ideas faster and easier. Everyday life also expands our mental sponge when we give ourselves stimulating experiences, but education does it much more quickly and efficiently. The more the mind-sponge is expanded by experience and education, the more knowledge it can absorb.

When you were first learning multiplication, you may have had a hard time picking it up. You may have felt that your "multiplication sponge," that part of your brain that was supposed to be picking up the finer points of multiplication, was soaked, but you somehow got by. Though you didn't know it then, just the act of learning your multiplication tables and solving math problems using multiplication was expanding your mind-sponge.

Then you graduated to the next level and found you had the same struggles understanding algebra. But when you thought back to multiplication, you realized how much better you now understood it. Your ability to understand multiplication improved because your comprehension sponge was larger from studying algebra. In other words, your brain's extra capacity made multiplication seem much simpler to you.

It follows that you will likely be an expert only in those topics with a lower level of complexity than the level you are trying next to conquer. That's why the best experts are researchers, only conquering topics as they look at the next complexity. The more your sons and daughters learn, the more they understand, even though thorough understanding may always seem as if it's one stage behind.

Those who understand the dry-sponge analogy and practice this principle never stop learning. For children, this analogy can encourage them to trust their education and desire more of it. It can do the same for parents while providing a tool that explains why their children should study algebra or chemistry even if they plan to major in political science.

Learning is the most exciting thing we will ever do. We tend to learn more about the things we enjoy. But stretching beyond those limits will expand our perspective, surprise us with new interests, and fill in the gaps of knowledge that would not have been filled otherwise, forever expanding our limitless, thirsty mind-sponge. Desiring knowledge and knowing how to learn is an essential life skill. Parents are key in establishing this desire in their children. As Socrates once said, "Education is kindling of a flame, not the filling of a vessel."

THE SALVES OF FORGIVENESS AND GRATITUDE

"Always forgive your enemies; nothing annoys them so much."
—Oscar Wilde

Forgiveness and gratitude are not inbred in most of us. These traits have to be learned, and some people never learn them. Young children who are taught forgiveness and gratitude can take advantage of their natural character traits much sooner than people like me who were largely self-taught. Living a life of forgiveness and gratitude becomes the salve to cure most tensions, self-delusions, and feelings of victimization, freeing up energy to use your traits and talents in a positive and constructive direction.

To teach forgiveness honestly, you must be forgiving. To teach gratitude with conviction, you must not have the aura of entitlement. If you are a father without these qualities, you need to pass this job over to Mom while you work on yourself.

As with everything, your opinions, attitudes, experiences, and prejudices will affect how you mentor as a father. *But don't hold yourself back with your perceived limitations.* You may not know etiquette like a blue blood, but you know basic manners. You may be clumsy dribbling a basketball, but you know how to bounce one. If you aren't a forgiving person, admit your shortcoming and show your children that you're striving to become so. If you find it difficult to be a grateful person, practice being grateful with your children when they show their love and affection to you. Your positive interaction and efforts will not only be noticed, but they will be instrumental in developing close relationships between you and your children.

> **DAD TIP:**
> *Certain attitudes and practices learned in our families can serve as a salve when our hearts—or those of others—are hurting. Some of these family-taught practices are forgiving, being grateful, not judging, respecting others, and always choosing kindness.*

Now that I've matured, I rarely, if ever, hold a grudge for long. As a Dad, it's important to be able to demonstrate this to your children. There are those I dislike and those I disagree with or don't understand. There is no one I actually hate or have ever hated.

I admit to being too impatient with things I don't understand, but I learned from my mom to never hold a grudge. Mom was a waitress during most of my childhood. She was a good one but never known for being a dynamo. Wonderfully kind to everyone, she is an exact and slower-paced person. She found that people can be demeaning and unkind to servers. She used to tell me that when people were rude, she would react by "killing them with kindness." It was her way of being in charge of the situation. She knew she might take the brunt for someone's bad day, but she refused to let people who mistreated her make her feel hurt or be unkind in return. She forgave them for their weaknesses, and it helped her be a better person. She may be slower-paced, but she is as sweet as Southern tea.

I didn't realize it until much later, but my mom also taught me gratitude. In tough times, when money was so scarce that choices had to be made between rent or food, my mom would tell me she was so thankful that all her kids were healthy. (She didn't mention that we were hell-raisers and uncooperative.)

Being grateful is rare enough when things are going right. Gratitude becomes more important when things are not going so well. It's an automatic mood lifter and shifts focus from troubles and victimization to possibilities and hope. Gratitude extended brings graciousness back to you.

"If you don't get everything you want, think of the things you don't get that you don't want."

—Oscar Wilde

BEING RESPECTFUL, NOT JUDGMENTAL, OF OTHERS

For four years while in the US Air Force, I lived near Mount Rushmore where Gutzon Borglum carved the faces of four US presidents on the side of a mountain. On the drive up to this national treasure, glimpses of it are around almost every turn. Its magnificence is unmistakable and inarguable. This one-of-a-kind monument is breathtaking, especially when you reflect on the skills of those who made it and the dangers they faced. It is perfect in our eyes as a national treasure. But if you look at it through binoculars, you will find cracks in the stone and details not so fine. But do we care? Of course not! We look at the total result that makes these small imperfections of no consequence at all.

So then why do we do just the opposite with ourselves and our fellow humans? For some reason, we take the small imperfections each of us has as humans and forget to measure them against the total work. Adopting this holistic perspective, you can understand that a supermodel and a worn-down housecleaner are both perfect as human beings. But we too often use our built-in binoculars to seek and find imperfections in others.

What if we took time to explain this expanded perspective to our young ones? What if we taught that the whole person is more than just the small parts that are contrary or critical? Would they not be just a little less judgmental about those of other races, faiths, abilities, and social skills, particularly those characteristics in which our fellow humans have little or no choice? Let the feelings your children may have felt when they themselves were being misjudged be assumed to have entered the hearts of those they may have judged unfairly. Most likely it will change their perspective.

BEING KIND TO OTHERS

"Kindness is the language which the deaf can hear and the blind can see."

—Mark Twain

Do you know the best way to teach your children how to show kindness to others? It's simply being kind to others yourself, and also being kind to your children. It is paramount that you be a good example for your children. If they see you being kind to others and helping those less fortunate, they will be more comfortable acting in that same way.

Never accept rude behavior from your kids toward you or anyone. To combat a habit of rudeness in your children early, provide opportunities for them to help others so they can experience the feeling of doing good. Praise them when they are kind or when they go out of their way to help someone.

Teach your children the art and habit of giving. They should know that a little burden on their part could be a huge benefit for someone else. After all, if everyone gave help and got help, we would all be better off. How and who your children help can be more effective if thought out and performed with grace. Being in a position to offer help to someone is therapeutic. And what you give comes back many times.

When I was eight or nine, I remember being bullied by two or three "tough" guys on a street near my home. I lived in a questionable neighborhood, and I was understandably nervous and scared about this confrontation. Then, suddenly, a city bus driver pulled up, opened his folding doors, and told the bullies to leave me alone. I really appreciated that but, of course, he had to keep to his schedule and move on. The bullies continued to harass me, but what happened next was a real surprise. The bus driver had driven around the block to check on me again. This time the bullies listened and left while I quickly scooted home.

I'll never forget the unselfish kindness of that young bus driver. I think of him and that incident often. He gave me an example of helping others that I will never forget: a black man in the late 1950s yelling at some white hooligans just to help me. He was a mentor to me, and I never knew who he was, but I will always remember his kindness.

RESPONSIBILITY AND CONSEQUENCES

One lesson feeds and complements other lessons. A vital key to the development of character and integrity is to teach your children responsibility and the meaning of facing consequences. I continue to bring up consequences because they are a necessary element for a balanced life.

A basic lesson in physics is, "for every action, there is a reaction." In life, wouldn't it be helpful if it were that clear! Feedback is a vital part of life, allowing you to adjust your ideas, thoughts, or behavior. When a mistake or bad choice is made, there should be a consequence—a lesson or penalty. If not, there is no learning nor correction.

Most of us think of consequences as a bad thing, but a consequence is nothing more than a result. A reward is a consequence also—a consequence of a job or act well done. Whether consequences are good or bad depends on many things, including desires, opinions, and outside influences, but mostly intent. Your child's intent will hopefully be to put forth an honest effort toward a noble goal. If a child's intent is honorable, a negative consequence should not involve guilt or punishment but rather be a worthwhile learning experience. While your actions are in your control, the results of those actions often are not. A good intention resulting in unforeseen results is a learning situation. Take your lesson and move on.

WINNING AND LOSING

Our children need to learn what it's like to win and to lose, and how to handle both. Failure is God's hand molding you. Winning is God's kiln, finishing what He and you have together molded. Too much losing will teach a child that he or she can never win, resulting in an expectation to lose or a choice to never try. Too much winning can mean a child is not being challenged and may become bored or overconfident. Too much losing will defeat a child. Too much winning may not prepare a child for the losses we all experience sooner or later.

> **DAD TIP:**
> *We must all take responsibility for our own actions, and from those actions—good or bad—will follow consequences. We must learn how to both win and lose graciously. And everyone must learn and practice humility, realizing that each person is equal, each is special.*

Some competitive fathers never let their children enjoy winning. If the children do perform well, it's not good enough, because they should have done better. These fathers think constant pressure or ridicule makes their children stronger and tougher. But sometimes it takes a victory to make them feel more confident, and these fathers should back off and allow their children to enjoy it. At the other extreme, fathers can sometimes make challenges too easy for their children or overly praise them. This can give the false impression that success comes easily (and we know it rarely does). Success is achieved by overcoming barriers; the barrier must be a tough but conquerable challenge.

TEACH HUMILITY

Humility is a great tool for balance. Just a little humility on your child's part will balance out the jealousy of others and foster admiration. However, egotism will negate others' favorable opinions of the otherwise wonderful qualities of your child. Being a uniquely talented or focused person is a special feeling. You and your children have a right to be proud when they are recognized as being outstanding at something, but don't allow yourself or your child to boast too much. A superior attitude is offensive and disrespectful of others.

We are all special in different but equal ways. Outside of our own egos, no one is more special than another. Some are smarter, more athletic, more beautiful, kinder, more understanding, more interesting, or more hilarious. But no one is more or less special than someone else in the world of relationships. This has to be taught, because it does not come naturally. If you want your child to feel special, the healthiest feeling they can have is that of self-confidence, not overconfidence.

We have all seen children be cruel to other children at school, at home, and at play. The odd duck is criticized or made fun of because they are different, and because those who do the name-calling and perform cruel jokes feel they are superior. It's been said that "kids will be kids," and that is absolutely true. But what is more accurate is "kids who have a mis-guided or inflated view of themselves will be the kind of kids who act in disregard toward others." When I see kids being cruel to other kids, I en-vision parents who do not understand how to help their children develop a good self-image without creating self-indulgent monsters. Then again, cruel children may act this way because they feel a need to inflate their ego due to a lack of self-worth at home. Help balance your child's vision of self. Recognize when to build it up and when to moderate it.

USING POSITIVE LANGUAGE

Being positive and using positive language is powerful and something you need to be conscious of. When you say, "Don't strike out," that nega-tive thought brings striking out to mind. Your words could be replaced by a positive statement, such as, "Keep your eye on the ball."

The reason for being positive is the great power of visualization. Im-ages created in the mind are as powerful as real images. If I told you *not* to think of a camel, what would happen? Did your camel have one hump or two? You did think of a camel, even if it was for a split second, didn't you? Encouragement through negatives such as *don't*, *never*, and *can't* are powerful influences in a way you might not anticipate, even if they were meant to be positive.

Some negative statements are unintended, and others are direct and unacceptable from a parent. We have all heard some parents say, "You're a brat!" or "You'll never amount to anything!" or "You'll never get a boyfriend if you don't lose weight!" *Never* say such negative and cruel words to your child. Always be positive and kind, yet firm. When your children misbehave, tell them their behavior needs to improve. You are condemning their behavior but not them. Be a positive influence and an encouraging role model. Turn those negative statements into positives: "Let's work on that behavior!" or "Let's try that one again; I know you can do better!" or "I am so proud of you for walking thirty minutes today!"

WILL YOUR HELP MAKE THEM STRONGER OR WEAKER?

When your kids need or request your help, it is critical to recognize the impact of your reaction. Consider when it's a good idea to help them or why they need the help. To help you decide, ask yourself this question: "If I help them, will it make them stronger or weaker?" You don't have to get analytical; just being aware of this question will help you do the right thing. Sometimes you may be helping them too much, and other times not enough. How do we know unless we look at how it impacts them? Let's look at the following scenarios as a male child grows up.

A Dad has an eleven-month-old boy learning to walk. The Dad helps him by letting the child hold his fingers while the child waddles along. Obviously, the Dad is making him stronger by exercising his legs and giving him some confidence and a sense of adventure. Later, the Dad doesn't let his child hold on. He stands a couple of feet away and encourages his son to come to him. Now he's helping his boy by teaching him confidence. At first, Dad's helping makes the child stronger; later, Dad's *not* helping makes him stronger.

When the child is in elementary school and asks his Dad for help with homework, of course the Dad responds. The father is helping when he explains concepts and methods to help his youngster understand. This makes his son stronger, smarter, and more confident. But if the Dad is doing the homework for him, he is not helping and is making his son weaker and dependent. His son may feel overloaded and frustrated trying to do it himself, but that's good training for adulthood. It's better to write his teacher a note stating you observed him working hard, but he didn't have time to finish. The teacher may need to know this.

The son is now sixteen and gets his first speeding ticket. He's upset, the Dad's upset, and the Dad may lecture him or listen to his excuses. But the Dad is not helping by paying his son's fine. Of course his son would think it would be a great help, but really it is making him weaker, or at least keeping him from getting stronger by learning responsibility. Children must learn to pay for their own mistakes. If they don't have money or a job, then assign them some work around the house to pay off the loan.

Well, now the boy is almost a man. He has learned many lessons in life from his father, and it is time for him to go to college. Should the Dad pay for his education? This depends on many factors, including the Dad's ability to afford it.

You should pay as much as is reasonable for your child's education. But what is considered reasonable? Beyond a parent's ability to pay is determining the real-world lessons that child may need to experience. Your children will need to know how to handle money, deal with pressure and stress, and balance their time. Placing some burden—financial, in this case—on them to deal with may be a good thing. Only involved parents will know how their child will react to too little or too much help.

An education makes anyone stronger and more independent. It's a gift your son or daughter will hopefully pass on to their children. I've told my son and two daughters not to expect an inheritance. They needed my help when they were young, had no money, and needed to find a way to earn a living on their own. So my children's inheritance came early in the form of teaching them self-reliance and my paying for their college education. Hopefully, they will still get an inheritance, but I'm not scrimping on my life to give them money they haven't earned and probably won't need if I've raised them correctly.

The child is now an adult, college educated, and asks the Dad for a loan. Now it gets more complicated. If it were you, would you give him a loan? Is it for a good reason? Will he pay you back? Are you able to do it? If you can do it, it comes back to the question, "Will this make him stronger or weaker?" If my son were asking, I would help if I could, but I would be sure to have him pay it back. You can always give him a gift, but that should always be your original idea and not a situation where you're letting him off the hook. And if he is unwise in his purchase (too large a home or too fancy a car), I would try to give him advice and help him not get into debt.

THINGS YOU SHOULD TEACH YOUR CHILDREN EARLY

Every child has varying strengths and weaknesses. As their father, you should know them. As an adult, you have already experienced success and failure. Knowing your children and your life experiences puts you in a special place to guide your children to become strong, confident people. While I had a strength in determination, I had many areas where I needed support. Having a more engaged father would have tremendously helped me to learn the following things much earlier than I did.

- I am not alone in having fears.
- Facing fear will dissolve it.
- No one else is any better than me ("better at," maybe, but "better than," no).
- Mistakes are okay. (Caveat: Knowingly doing wrong is not a mistake.)
- You can't wait for others to move forward.
- You *always* have choices (this was a big one for me).

- Character and integrity are vitally important.
- Develop the joy and beauty of imagination. (With his stories of travel, my dad did help me with this.)
- Decisions made for security are not the same decisions you would make for freedom (growth).
  - » For example, determining to run a lemonade stand is a choice for freedom, but deciding you are too shy to sell lemonade is a choice for security. Similarly, going to college in your hometown is a secure choice, while enrolling in a school across the country is a choice for freedom.

Be a father who has a simple plan to listen to and learn about his children, who has a philosophy to teach his children about how life should be lived.

BUILDING STRONG SONS AND DAUGHTERS

Building strong sons and daughters is difficult, demanding, and highly rewarding. It certainly takes effort and caring to do it in a way that will work best for each of your children. They are all different in temperament and ability. One important difference lies in your child's gender. Boys and girls have different, gender-specific needs, and as Dads we must be sensitive to those needs. We will discuss this in the next chapter.

YOUR ROAD MAP: CHAPTER 10

Start: Building strong children, those who have self-confidence and compassion for others, begins the first time you hold your child. They watch every move you make and every mood you bring to each day. You are your child's first and best example.

Major Highway: Realize that your example, your teaching, and your mentoring can make or break your child's character. Children who grow up accepting responsibility within a family where mistakes are allowed will become mature adults who do not fear responsibility or failure. They are comfortable with the axiom: "If at first you don't succeed, try, try again."

On the Open Road: Every child deserves balance in his or her life. In what ways do you help your children, no matter what their age, develop balance in their lives?

Tenth Stop: Consider the multitude of positive character traits that have been discussed in this chapter and how you can help build these in your children. Helping them set and meet goals is one of the sweetest gifts you can offer your children; doing the work for them is one of the least helpful things you can do.

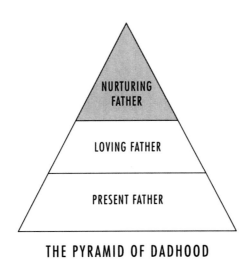

THE PYRAMID OF DADHOOD

THE PINNACLE OF
THE
PYRAMID

CHAPTER 11

NURTURING SONS AND DAUGHTERS

"You are the bows from which your children as living arrows are sent forth."

—Kahlil Gibran, *The Prophet*

Being present, loving, and nurturing are the answers to being a successful father. But within those parameters are details that can't be ignored when dealing with sons or daughters. And while most interactions will be similar, you represent a different image and have a different role with a son versus with a daughter.

FATHER HUNGER

Have no doubt that a son and daughter suffer in varying degrees when denied the mentoring of their father. While girls need fatherly love and an example of male propriety, boys most need the example of masculinity their fathers provide. A passage in Frank Pittman's *Man Enough* sums it up nicely:

> Life for most boys and many grown men is a frustrating search for the lost father who has not yet offered protection, provision, nurturing, modeling, or, especially, anointment. All those tough guys who want to scare the world into seeing them as men, and who fill up the jails; all those men who aren't at home, who don't know how to be a man with a woman, only a brute or a boy, and who fill up the divorce courts; all those corporate raiders and rain-forest burners and war starters who want more in hopes that more will make them feel better; and all those masculopathic philanderers, contenders, and controllers who fill up my office—all of them are suffering from Father Hunger.

Or as stated in *The Good Father* by Mark O'Connell: "Social deprivation, injurious life experiences, and hurtful relational interactions generate aggression." And further, "Nurture and social context unarguably play a major role [in aggression]."

We all know men and boys who fall into this description. I see them among my friends, coworkers, and even my extended family. As for me, my father hunger took me in a different direction, one that pulls many of us into a different paradigm of acceptance and validation. Instead of false bravado, I had no bravado. As a child, I was meek and suspicious of other males. I was soft and knew it, but I didn't know how to get out of it. I needed my father for this, and he rarely gave me the lessons, the backbone, or the confidence to shake it.

My dad once gave me support and direction in the only way he knew how. I was under a highway viaduct where a couple of punks were harassing me. My dad came upon the scene in his car and stopped. I was relieved, because I was about to get my butt kicked. But instead of chasing the boys away, he said only one boy could fight me, not both. I understood from this incident that he wanted me to stand up for myself. My resulting black eye and bloody nose hurt, but my self-esteem felt temporarily healed and I was proud to have faced my fear. My mother was furious that he let it happen, but I loved him for it—not because he handled it the right way, but because he stopped to help me, and I needed his attention.

DAD TIP:
Even a father who is present can be "missing" in the eyes of his children. Unless he spends time nurturing, teaching, setting a positive example, and simply showing love for his children, his presence may still not fill their needs.

A SON IS A REFLECTION OF HIS FATHER'S IMAGE

"Manhood is mimesis. To be a man, a boy must see a man."
—J. R. Moehringer, *The Tender Bar*

Both sons and daughters need the love of their father. But what boys need that girls do not is an example of how to be male and eventually a man. A son reflects his father's image in some way, whether it be good or bad.

Some fathers are like concave mirrors: their son's reflection is concentrated into a single beam that says, "Be what I am, do what I do, think how I think; my way is the right way." Other fathers are like convex mirrors that diffuse their son's reflection and send one of these messages: "I don't have time," "I don't care," "I'll get to it later," or "You are on your own." But the best fathers are what I would call ideal mirrors for their son's image. They are perfect planes reflecting a true and unbiased image, a clear reflection where concern and caring are not reflected away nor are the father's biases sharply focused. A son can see and know his true self with the help of his father. We men, we fathers and our sons, are never perfect. We must be aware of our limitations and work to overcome them.

When the father isn't present, the boy must find a fatherly image somewhere else, and perfect reflections are hard to find. Often a boy will see himself through influences such as gangs, which are like carnival mirrors where your image is severely twisted and contorted and not the true you. Neither can mothers be ideal mirrors for their sons. Those mirrors would be clouded and hazy. After all, mothers cannot reflect what it means to be a man.

BOYS WANT THEIR FATHERS TO BE THEIR HEROES, NOT SUPERHEROES

In *Man Enough*, Pittman states:

> There was no secret to fathering, no magical answers about masculinity that are passed on from generation to generation. Boys learn to be men by being with their fathers, experiencing the world and living life. But if they haven't had that experience, they may never feel comfortable with an awareness of what it means to be a man, what they are supposed to do with their masculinity, and how they can become fathers themselves.

It takes a lot for a boy to hate his father. Even when he is convinced that his father is not a good man, or even perhaps an evil man, he is still fascinated by him. If the father is absent, a boy will dream of a male image that he imagines is there for him.

I recently met a man from Jamaica, whom I'll call George, who works where I sometimes write. Our conversation that day turned to his father, who was not there for him when he was growing up in Jamaica, and it hurt him deeply. Later, someone told him his father had given him up so George could escape the ghetto, where young men like him were often killed or maimed. He beamed when he got to the part of the story where his father had sacrificed him to save him. George needed to know his father loved him, protected him, and most important, did not turn his back on him. A father is important even when he is not around.

Ask one hundred young men whether they identify with Bruce Willis in the movie *Die Hard* or Steve Martin in the movie *Parenthood*, and my guess is ninety-nine would pick Bruce Willis—not too surprising or un-natural. Fatherhood is not as glamorous as being an action hero. When a boy has an involved and capable father, a Dad, he may have heroes outside his family, but he is not as driven by them. Boys without fathers, however, are left unchecked, not having real men like the Steve Martin character to show them what being a real man is about.

Image is important to us males. We want to be respected as masculine beings, and for the most part, the masculine image is misrepresented by the entertainment industry. Boys without real-life mentors buy into this false image because young men raised without a father have difficulty identifying their masculine self. They feel they have to prove themselves, but to whom?

Often a young man will measure himself against other young men raised without involved fathers, or he dreams of being like one of his hypermasculine movie heroes. Comparisons like these place a value on toughness, aggression, and violence, with little or no regard for compas-sion, compromise, and kindness, which are considered signs of weakness in that make-believe, hypermasculine world.

Males often compete for the macho image of being with and having their way with women. The young women who bear these boys' children are often fatherless also, seeking male approval because they had none at home. The basis for this kind of relationship is tissue thin, and there will be no happy family. So the cycle continues. We have a fatherless boy wanting to prove his manhood and a fatherless girl seeking male approv-al, resulting in a child born with little chance of having a life with both a mother and a father, resulting in more fatherless children, often leading to more violence, more poverty, and more social upheaval.

I wanted to love my father, and I did, but he did such despicable things to my mother, to his children, and to himself. He turned his back on us, cussed at us, sometimes apologized to us, and did it all over again. How could I want this man to be my hero? But I did. I can't think of anything particular I needed him to do. He didn't have to be a star baseball player or a doctor. He didn't need to cure cancer or build skyscrapers. I just wanted my dad around as a sober, caring man. That alone would have made him my hero.

> **DAD TIP:**
> *Being a Dad doesn't mean being a superhero or even anyone out of the ordinary. Being a Dad means showing your son how to be male and how to be a loving and kindhearted husband and father, and being present to help your son answer questions about his self-identity as he progresses through life.*

As a dad, ask yourself if you are being the person you wish to be for your son. You can't tell him to do one thing and then do the opposite yourself. Boys need their dads to be examples of not only how to be men, but how to properly treat women. They need to know when to stand their ground and when to let things go. Dads need to teach boys how to throw a baseball. I can almost always tell when a boy has never played catch with his father. I can't recall ever playing catch with mine. I'm now a grandfather and still wish I had that experience.

Dads need to be there to answer the questions boys don't want to ask their mothers. And when they themselves become dads, they will look back on how they were raised for answers. Don't let their conclusions regarding fatherhood be the wrong ones. Real heroes do not wear capes, nor do they necessarily run fast or shoot straight. Real superheroes are nurturing people who take personal and family responsibility head on.

A FATHER IS A MODEL OF CONFIDENCE

> *"I teach my sons to look everyone they talk with directly in the eye. I tell them to hold their heads erect, speak confidently and with a strong voice."*
>
> —Earl Ofari Hutchinson,
> *Black Fatherhood: The Guide to Male Parenting*

How to interact with others is a lesson Dr. Hutchinson gave to his sons that all young men need to be taught. And even though he didn't mention it in his quote, I'm sure he would include being respectful. Respect is an aspect that may be missing if Hutchinson's words were learned from the wrong source, such as a gang or misguided friends. As a boy and young man, I rarely looked people in the eye and never spoke confidently or with a strong voice. I know firsthand that lacking this confidence made me invisible to many people. My father knew I was a meek kid, but he didn't really do anything to get me out of my shell.

I do recall, by its uniqueness, his advice to "swing your arms when you walk," and I did. It was something he noticed that I didn't. It's not *what* you teach your child that is primary; it's that you are involved and teaching. It's not the advice you give so much as it is that you care enough to give advice. It is more important to do what you say than to say what you'll do.

I can see that my son, Mike, has quite a bit of me in him. This is neither good nor bad—it's who we are. We've both struggled with confidence, we both like baseball, and we both have experience as military pilots. He had a male role model to guide him, and that was me. Who could have been a better model for him than his own father? Better yet, what man could have cared as much about him as me? A man does not have to be perfect to be the best mentor for his son.

> **DAD TIP:**
> *It's not* what *you teach your child that is primary; it's that you are involved and teaching. It's not the advice you give so much as it is that you care enough to give advice. It is more important to* do *what you say than to say what you'll do. Action is the key.*

QUICK NOTES ON BOYS

- Mentor them; show them what real-life men are like.

- Do guy things together.
- Teach them to be respectful.
- Know their friends.
- Let them try new things with your supervision (e.g., fix a flat tire).
- Let them approach you with problems.
- Never shame them!

DAD TIP:

Who better than a boy's father to be his male role model? Being a Dad means getting involved with your son, knowing his strengths and weaknesses, and accepting him as he is while showing him ways to grow in confidence, respect, and self-esteem.

YOU ARE THE FIRST MAN IN YOUR DAUGHTERS' LIVES

"The most important person in a young girl's life? Her father."
—Meg Meeker, *Strong Fathers, Strong Daughters*

An excellent book for all men with daughters is *Strong Fathers, Strong Daughters* by Meg Meeker, a pediatrician who is an expert on treatment of adolescents with medical and social problems. She writes:

> I have watched daughters talk to their fathers. When you [their fathers] come in the room, they change. Everything about them changes: their eyes, their mouths, their gestures, their body language. Daughters are never lukewarm in the presence of their fathers. They may take their mother for granted, but not you. They light up—or they cry. They watch you intensely. They hang on your words. They wait for your attention, and they wait for it in frustration—or in despair. They need a gesture of approval, a nod of encouragement, or even simple eye contact to let them know you care and are willing to help.

174

Having raised two daughters, I find everything in Dr. Meeker's book to be helpful and true in my own experience. Men have a special relationship with their daughters and even more special responsibilities. Meeker's book will awaken you to the power, importance, and wonderful purpose you have in being a responsible father to a young woman. The statistics and data she presents regarding young women's career success, on unwed pregnancy, and on other important topics emphasize the positive impact of responsible fathering and would convince any man of his significant influence in the life of his daughter.

TREAT DAUGHTERS WITH LOVE AND RESPECT

Father-daughter relationships are powerful and unique, which can be either good or bad. No one has the ear of a young woman like her father. She will believe what he says, whether complimentary or degrading. She may not realize she believes it, but she does.

A father is the first man in her life. He is the first man she tries to impress, and she never stops trying. All men are compared to you. You may rarely understand her, and she may rarely understand you, but there are critical moments in your relationship that will help her self-image, her delicate psyche, and her self-respect. Be there for her. She learns confidence and self-esteem from the way you interact with and treat her.

SPENDING TIME TOGETHER

"It is admirable for a man to take his son fishing, but there is a special place in heaven for the father who takes his daughter shopping."

—John Sinor

I didn't take my daughters shopping often, but from the time they were born I spent time with them whenever I could. The one thing I know I did and still do for my daughters is to let them know I love them. I recall a winter morning when my family was visiting a friend in the Ozarks. I wanted to photograph a sunrise in this beautiful area. My daughter April was nine or ten years old, and she showed an interest in going along. I was happy she wanted to join me. When I woke her the next morning, it was cold and dark outside. It didn't seem so much fun to get up this early from a warm comfortable bed, but she did.

We dressed, trying not to awaken anyone, and left our friend's small cottage, welcomed by a fresh snow that was just perfect for photography. We drove to a spot I had scouted and waited for the sunrise to come. I misjudged the timing, so it was still dark and we waited for the sun, talking and drinking our orange juice from McDonald's. The sunrise came, and it was beautiful. I took photos for the next hour or two with April patiently trudging behind in the tracks I left in the snow. I still have those photos, but I don't have to look at them to remember that special time with April. She remembers it also, highlighted by her spilling orange juice all over the seat of my new car. A special morning for our relationship, it created memories that are ours alone.

> ## DAD TIP:
> *We Dads raise our daughters to have the same manners, respect for others, and self-confidence as we teach to our sons, but the teaching is done in a different way. Tone of voice, word choice, and heart-to-heart listening are different in your interactions with your daughters than they might be with your sons. That's important to remember.*

Now that my children are grown, I'm still trying to stay connected. My older daughter, April, went to football and baseball games with me before she became a busy mom, and now we try to have lunch once a month. My younger daughter, Rachel, and I plan to run a half-marathon together. We also enjoy hiking in the state park behind our home. My son, Mike, has been away in the Army for a few years, but I follow his career closely and visit him whenever possible. When he comes home, we try to play golf or just hang out together. I love these times with my grown children. It keeps us close, and you couldn't pay me a billion dollars to give it up.

A DAUGHTER NEEDS YOUR PROTECTION, LOVE, AND IMAGE OF MANHOOD

"A son is a son 'til he takes him a wife; a daughter is a daughter all of her life."

—Irish saying

I don't take this Irish saying literally, but it underscores the special responsibilities a father feels for his daughters. Who will protect your daughters if you don't? Intuitively, fathers protect their daughters in ways mothers can't. They give a feeling of comfort that mothers can't, through masculinity and strength. They need a male figure to look up to and to show them they are worthy of male love. And they need you to provide the image of a real man: a man who has respect for women, who has a balanced temperament, and who is wise, helpful, and loving. No man can do this quite like a father. Who she marries will be influenced mightily by you.

The social implications of having no father are tragic. In an article entitled "Long-Term Effects of Divorce on Children," author Neil Kalter states:

> Girls whose parents divorce may grow up without the day-to-day experience of interacting with a man who is attentive, caring and loving. The continuous sense of being valued and loved as a female seems an especially key element in the development of the conviction that one is indeed femininely lovable. Without this regular source of nourishment, a girl's sense of being valued as a female does not seem to thrive.

Fathers nourish their daughters by protecting them. Protecting your daughters will involve everything from being strict and firm to being warm and understanding. Many times the father will be "hated" by his daughter for doing what is right for her. Do what you must anyway—she doesn't really hate you. She's really tricking herself, and you, to see if you really care enough to be engaged in her life. Her ego may actually be angry, but her real being will feel love and protection. The ego's anger will fade, and your daughter's love will grow. This is difficult to believe sometimes, but if you are not unreasonable in your demands and really show concern for her, no amount of proper interference will ever harm your relationship.

But beware your daughters! They can wrap you around their finger. Don't think when you give in to their charms that you are gaining favor or doing the right thing. Their safety is so much more important than your being their pal. Actually, they will often brag about how you keep a tight rein on them.

STAGES OF PROTECTION

Protecting your daughter is a play with three acts. Act I is "Safety First." Your infant, then toddler daughter is protected by you and her mother emotionally and physically—rarely is she out of your sight. You watch strangers closely; you hold her hand tightly; your radar is always on for signals of danger. No one and nothing will hurt your little girl. Her needs are met. Her health is protected.

Later, in Act II, "Limits," daughters become more independent. By the time they are preteens, things get complicated. Your daughters want to be accepted so much that they may do things and allow things to happen that are not in their best interests, and because of this you must continue to protect them. Rules set for them are to be strictly followed, such as don't talk to strangers; don't be alone anywhere out of the home, especially at night; tell a parent where you are at all times; don't chat with anyone on the Internet you don't know, and so on.

There's a lot of pressure on young girls to be popular with their peers and with boys. They are taught how to do this by the media and marketing gurus—in all the wrong ways. You must counter these impressions that they have to be skinny, provocative, dressed in name brands, sexy, and more. Only you can offset the media blitz and misleading information.

Explain to your daughters the perceived threats that you envision, your rules, and why they exist. The best way to protect your daughters does not involve locking them indoors or threatening severe punishment. The best way is to teach them self-respect and a solid knowledge of right from wrong, truth from fiction. Because you can't be this vigilant forever.

In Act III, "Flying Solo," they will have to be their own person and do things on their own. By then, they must have absorbed the basic skills and knowledge to be aware of dangerous situations and to protect themselves. As a Dad, you are the one person, especially the one male, who can give your daughter the power of her own convictions. Just a simple show of concern and love will let her know there is someone who already accepts her as she is and will convince her that pleasing herself and making her parents proud is paramount over pleasing those who show just passing interest—protecting her from unhealthy relationships, or pleasing others for the wrong reasons.

DON'T OVERPROTECT!

You can overdo protection, just like anything can be overdone. Protecting daughters comes much more naturally than protecting sons, but don't protect your daughter from learning how to handle everyday life. She must learn to deal with difficult people and aggressive men because you will not always be there to help.

Our daughters must realize that disappointments are a part of life that can be overcome. Young women must understand that acting as a victim is harmful and weak, but rising from disappointment and taking charge of their life is strength. Let them fight their way out of problems with your oversight. You can't treat a daughter like she's everyone's princess. She's just your princess, a princess with rules and moxie. Know to step in when it appears she needs confidence and support, and know when to quietly back off. Be wise in your interventions.

TWO WORDS A FATHER NEVER WANTS TO HEAR IN THE SAME SENTENCE

Sex is a frightening topic when it involves your daughter. Yes, I put the two words *sex* and *daughter* in the same sentence. We can't stick our heads in the sand about this topic—your daughter is a human being who will eventually have a natural inclination toward sex. The best you can do for her is to help ensure that she respects her body and has a huge dose of self-esteem. Hopefully, Mom will help with this encouragement and all the details. But as a man, you have unique credibility and perspective regarding this topic.

Here's a sobering fact I heard on *NBC Evening News*: fifty percent of women between the ages of twenty and twenty-four are infected, through sexual contact, with human papillomavirus (HPV), which is the main cause of cervical cancer. Your daughter must hear from you, her male role model, what I'm about to say.

DAD TIP:

Often as dads—even "capital-D" Dads—we chicken out when it's time to talk with our daughters about sex. We want to leave it to Mom. But we can talk with them about self-respect, sexual safety, and the mutual respect that occurs when two people in love don't rush into sexual activity. The most important message to convey to your daughter is that you love and accept her, and that you will be there for her no matter what. She will then feel free to discuss anything with you.

When your daughter's boyfriend wants to have sex too early in their relationship, there is no doubt that his hormones and ego really and desperately do. But if he really cares for her and is truly a mature, decent, and loving person, his heart hopes she will turn him down. He will love and respect her more for it. This message from a mother will not have quite the same impact as hearing it from a Dad.

GUIDANCE FOR HER RELATIONSHIPS

Objecting to a current boyfriend is like throwing gasoline on a fire. The real way to influence your daughter about whom she dates is to give her some traits to look for in a boy before she becomes involved with him. I suggest you choose three characteristics for her to look for that you think are the most important, and then pass these on to her.

Some suggested characteristics are being kind to others, being responsible, being liked by others, doing well in school, and being considerate, caring, and consistent. Whichever characteristics you choose, be sure to put the thoughts in her head early so she is looking for these traits *before* getting involved with a boy. Expressing these characteristics to her will help prove that any objections you may have in the future about a boyfriend are not personal but based on the boy's lack of these traits.

Sometimes the attention a girl gets from a boy is so wanted or needed that she will readily overlook or even be blind to the negative aspects of the boy or the relationship. This is especially true of fatherless girls, and it happens over and over again. I know many women who did not have fatherly love, and they have struggled and suffered in their relationships with men. So have their daughters, and so too will their granddaughters, until one of them chooses a decent man who will be a responsible father.

THE BOTTOM LINE REGARDING DAUGHTERS

The bottom line is that you must be the example of the things your daughter will look for in other men. You must be vigilant and protect her from herself and others, as much as is practical. Your guidance and example will dramatically determine the course of her life.

Instill pride and self-esteem in your daughter, and especially give her your love to keep her safe as she goes out on her own in a world full of predators. Always be there for her and let her know you want to help. Do everything you can to keep your daughter from becoming another statistic related to sex, divorce, drugs, mental problems, or depression. You will likely be successful if you just try.

Girls who have loving fathers have a greater understanding of the male-female relationship and have much more confidence in themselves and their sexuality. They are not nearly as likely to seek male approval by ingratiating themselves to men through sexual promiscuity. You may find that what your daughters think of you as a father will show up in the men they marry. When those men reflect your values, it is an indication that your daughters appreciate how you raised them.

QUICK NOTES ON GIRLS

- Know their friends, especially the boys.
- Watch your innocent comments about how they look or dress, which are always taken seriously.
- Set reasonable but clear boundaries for them. They need space, but not too much.
- They love to be hugged, usually when their friends aren't around. But do it then, too.
- Treat them with the respect you expect others to have for them.
- Trust your gut when it comes to their safety. Protect them.

DAD TIP:

Spending time with your daughter is just as important as spending time with your son. If she likes baseball, take her to a game. If she likes fishing, take her with you and teach her how to bait her hook. If she likes shopping or movies, take her to the mall or to see the latest release. It doesn't matter what you do; it matters that you have father-daughter time together, doing something you both enjoy. And if you don't particularly like what she enjoys, pretend. It's the time together that counts.

A FATHER IS A MENTOR

A classic role for a father is as a mentor to his children, especially to his sons. A mentor shows the way for someone less experienced. Does that sound like a Dad to you? You can improve your mentoring skills by simply being conscious of your children's need for mentoring and by following through. Much of what you do as a mentor will come naturally, but you also have a lot of resources to help you.

One important resource for most of us is our own parents. There are also in-laws, grandparents, friends, and others, but they won't all have the same opinions or advice. You must sort through that advice and think what would work for you and your children. Of course there are magazines about parenting, but the publishers know men are not likely to read them and therefore don't write as much to fathers. Before it was bought by *Parents* magazine and no longer published, *Parenting* magazine had the tag line: "What Matters to Moms."

While I don't read parenting magazines either, I can read just about anything and relate it to being a Dad. I especially recommend self-help books, spiritual books, educational books, and memoirs. These books may not talk specifically about being or having a father, but you can extend what they teach into how and what you teach your children.

As fathers, we are responsible for ensuring the best possible future for our children. Nurturing them represents more than a passive interest in them. It involves tailoring your parenting, not only to their sex, but also to their needs, strengths, and weaknesses. Be there when they need you!

YOUR ROAD MAP: CHAPTER 11

Start: Nurturing your children is one of your most vital roles as a Dad. Even though we want to develop the same self-respect and self-confidence in both our sons and our daughters, we must be aware that the pathways to doing so are not the same for both.

Major Highway: One of the most important ways to discover what to teach our children and how to nurture them is to watch them interact with others. Do they look people in the eye when they speak? Do they walk with confidence? Do they show compassion? Teaching these things to our daughters and our sons may be done in different ways, but it is vital that both learn these life-enhancing traits.

On the Open Road: If you had only one day to help mold your child into the person you want him or her to be, what aspects of their character would you concentrate on, and what approach would you take? Would you show love? Would you teach? Would you demonstrate by example?

Eleventh Stop: As Dads, we love, teach, and nurture our sons and daughters differently. Review the Quick Notes about sons and daughters and see how these fit into your life as a Dad, or imagine how you will want them to fit into your life when you become more than a father—when you choose to be a Dad.

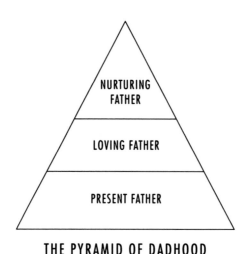

THE PYRAMID OF DADHOOD

```

# MONEY VERSUS SUC-CESS

*"Success is to be measured not so much by the position that one has reached in life as by the obstacles which he has overcome."*

—Booker T. Washington

Your responsibilities as a Dad do not fly out the door when your children do. Don't assume they know how to handle what you have handled for them in the past. If you've properly prepared them you can relax a bit, but be vigilant. Be sure they can handle money, success, and failure on their own, and continue to give advice when they need it. If you've always been there for them before, they will listen.

## IS MONEY SUCCESS?

You might think this chapter's title, "Money versus Success," is odd be-
```

cause so many people—too many, really—think of success as having money. But the very purpose of this chapter is to separate the two while emphasizing how to teach your children to handle both. While money, or its usefulness, is often a factor in success, it is just one of several defining factors. *You don't need money to be successful, and you can have money and be unsuccessful.* Other aspects of success will be discussed later in this chapter.

It is perfectly natural and sensible for all of us to desire success and money. Despite the association between these two goals, kids must neither assume that money will symbolize their success nor that success will necessarily bring them money. In some occupations, such as sales, income is synonymous with success. But the successes of many people in honorable and necessary professions cannot be measured by their incomes. It would be unfair, in determining success, to compare the salary of a talented and successful teacher, or enlisted military personnel, to the salary or commission of a talented and successful salesperson. You can only say they are both successful in being good at what they do.

DAD TIP:

Try to separate the concepts of money and success. You don't need money to be successful, and you can have money but be unsuccessful and unhappy. The important thing is to teach our kids the place of money in their lives.

Children must understand that personal value is not measured by the value of tangible belongings. Our value is measured in our reach to do 'good' for our families, ourselves, and others, and in the depth to which we do it.

Anyone with a significant and positive impact is a success in any society. Sometimes that involves money, but often it does not. Money is generally a temporary fix, while actions, such as teaching and healing, have a more permanent effect. As we discussed earlier in this book, teaching a man to fish is much more valuable than giving him a fish to eat. My wife's success or value as a parent educator is not reflected in her income. She touches people's lives in positive and permanent ways that can never have a price put on them. Like a parent educator, many occupations help others not just in the moment, but also in the days and years ahead.

Some people have inherited family fortunes and live a great lifestyle but have done little or nothing to contribute to society. They appear successful to many because of their clothing, cars, homes, education, or appearance, but they may not be nearly as successful as, say, an occupational therapist, a college counselor, a teacher, or a soldier. We tend to compare ourselves, right or wrong, to those we think more fortunate. Those of us who don't do this *are* fortunate.

While Mother Teresa, for example, had a tremendously successful life without any tangible rewards, those who inherit wealth and use their money solely to indulge their selfish desires and whims can hardly be called a success. So stating that money does not necessarily equal success, nor does success necessarily equal money, is beyond argument. Your children certainly need to understand this.

While the money we earn does not always reflect the success in our lives, there is nothing inherently wrong with having money. I love getting, winning, finding, and especially earning and saving money. We've always heard that money cannot buy happiness, and this is certainly true. But having enough money and resources to take care of your family can bring you much peace.

Though we may have been taught that the love of money is evil, money itself is certainly not evil. Some ways people get money and some things they spend it on are evil, but money itself, or financial success, is nothing to be ashamed of. *The proper handling of and attitude toward money are vital lessons that need to be taught to your children.*

WHEN AND HOW TO TEACH THE VALUE OF MONEY

Most children do not judge their parents by how much money they have, especially when they are very young. Thank goodness for that! Money to them is just something you pull out of your pocket or wallet when you need it. Their lack of understanding of the value of money is not a problem for a while, but eventually they need to learn that money is not magic green paper that turns frowns into ice cream smiles.

When my older daughter, April, first started babysitting, she would leave five- and ten-dollar bills lying around the house or leave them in her pockets to be found later in the wash. I recognized that she had no idea of the value of that money, and I got on her a few times to be more careful with it. It didn't seem to help. April continued to treat money as if it were lint from her pockets.

Her attitude toward money changed only when babysitting became more work than fun and after the realization that being able to buy things she wanted was easier than asking for them and being denied. She then became much more responsible with her hard-earned money. My lesson was reinforced when she could relate it to her personal experience and her personal experience reminded her of my lesson.

When your children are old enough to understand what money is, begin familiarizing them with its value and convince them that it doesn't secretly breed in your pockets. Every greenback and every coin is a representation of hard work or a special skill, and you get it by working or creating.

If children are given money without earning it, they'll never understand how hard some people have to work to get it. So make a deal with them when they ask for something they want. Give them a chore or chores that are worth enough money to pay for what they want. They will appreciate their purchase more, most likely take better care of it, and become more discerning about what they want.

> **DAD TIP:**
> *We Dads can offer a different approach to teaching children the value of money. While the chores kids do as part of their daily lives are often under Mom's watch, Dads can come up with "special" chores to help children learn about earning.*

FINANCIAL SUCCESS IS EARNING, NOT GETTING

Anyone would agree that winning the lottery would be pretty exciting. You could do things you've only dreamed of and hopefully help others. But winning the lottery is not success, nor is finding money in the street or having blue eyes.

Good fortune is not the same thing as earning a fortune. No skill, hard work, dedication, perseverance, discipline, or intelligence is involved in good fortune. Now that doesn't mean a lottery winner cannot become a success with the intelligent use of this newfound wealth, but unfortunately many lottery winners do not become successful nor are they really happier after a few years of having a lot of money. They were given a "school of fish," but they didn't know what to do with it. Once the fish were gone, luck would not bring them back again.

Success has more to do with how you are valued or what you do with your earnings than by how much money you have. And sometimes, as we've established, success has nothing at all to do with money, as proven by those whose success comes through love and hard work as well as appreciation from others.

Earned money is the reward and acknowledgment of your value as a contributor, and your worth lies in your realized potential. Success is being happy and maximizing your value to help others. Sometimes money can help you do this—it is a great tool that can help make your life better. Put your children in a position to earn it honestly, handle it well, and remember it as a tool of commerce and not necessarily a symbol of success or happiness.

LET THEM LEARN TO EARN

"The only lasting favor which the parent may confer upon the child is that of helping the child to help itself."
—Napoleon Hill

My wife and I did not provide our kids with an unearned allowance. Neither did we give an allowance for routine work around the house. We weren't trying to be cheapskates or unfair, it's just that when you are a family, you work together.

Our kids were expected to clean their rooms, help take out the trash, put away dishes, and more. Not all work in life is rewarded with money. Your children need to understand that some of the work they perform is rewarded by having a clean home, good food, self-respect, and healthy relationships. If they don't understand that, then the reward is a happier, more generous Mom and Dad.

> **DAD TIP:**
> *Consider having your children earn their allowances, not for routine household chores that are a part of living together as a family, but for special, out-of-the-ordinary jobs that are accomplished with preset standards that must be met.*

But don't think of your kids as built-in slaves. Some jobs around the house, perhaps cleaning out gutters or power-washing the deck, are more demanding and deserve a little compensation. These bigger jobs could be rewarded by cash, teaching them that the money they receive is the result of hard work.

Nothing is wrong with a small allowance if it is earned honestly. Eventually, they will be cautious in their purchases because what they buy will be related to their efforts in getting it. An unearned allowance is a misleading lesson suggesting money is a privilege and not a reward.

MONEY LESSONS FOR OLDER CHILDREN

Before I get into how to teach your older children how to handle money, I have two warnings. First, if you have never been successful with money decisions, don't pass your habits on to your kids. Get help if you need it for both you and them. There are many books to help you and them discuss and learn about handling money. I recommend *Rich Dad, Poor Dad for Teens* by Robert Kiyosaki.

Second, kids are different, even in the same family. One child may get pleasure from spending and displeasure from saving. Another may get pleasure from saving and be miserly in spending. Neither situation is ideal. The first child could one day get into financial problems, and the second child could have issues with enjoying life or keeping friends. As always, balance is the key. Help your children learn a balance between spending and saving. If you've given them opportunities to earn their own money and buy their own things, you'll be able to recognize their habits of spending long before they have credit cards.

There are some basic rules that can get your kids off to an excellent start with good money habits. I gave my children the following advice when they started earning their own money as adults.

1. Don't spend all that you make. Set aside money for your savings and emergencies. Build your wealth so you have enough when you retire. Measure the expense of something as a percentage of your net worth (assets minus debts)—not a percentage of what you earn. An unnecessary $1,000 purchase is not affordable just because you make $2,000 a month. If you owe $20,000 more than you're worth, you cannot afford that kind of spending.

2. Meet all your financial obligations first, and then look to have fun with the rest of the money—money not set aside for savings and emergencies. Budget a certain percentage of your income for guilt-free fun. It would be foolish to live a lifestyle where fun is not affordable. This often happens to young families that buy a house so

expensive they have nothing left for anything else.

3. After you have an emergency fund, start saving and investing. Get investment advice from someone financially knowledgeable and trustworthy, for free if possible. But it may be worth a fee (not a commission) to get professional investment advice based on your circumstances and risk tolerance. You'll get straight advice with a fee. With commissions, salespeople have an incentive to sell you products you may not need. Those products may not be right for you. And avoid "load" funds. A load is when part of your purchase is used to pay a commission and, therefore, is not available to buy shares. No-load funds are just as capable as load funds, and they don't cost you a percentage of your investment.

4. Never touch your savings without using it for what you had planned. Use your emergency funds for emergencies, usually an amount equal to at least three months' salary, and replace it as soon as possible after an emergency.

5. Get a credit rating early. You can do this by simply buying necessities, like gas and groceries, on a credit card. But be especially careful to pay the total on the card each month. If you can't afford something, then don't buy it. This is a simple but powerful lesson to burn into your young brain. Credit card companies deluge college students with preapproved credit cards because they know students are backed by their parents. But after college, if you haven't established credit, you will find it difficult to get a credit card or a loan without a cosigner. This happened to a twenty-eight-year-old young man who paid cash or used a debit card for everything until his father advised him to use a credit card to build his credit rating. Predictably, he was denied a credit card until he proved he had many times more in savings than the limit on his requested credit card. A good credit rating will get you a lower interest rate on borrowed money. And we, your parents, will be happy not to be on the hook for your debts as cosigners.

These are some of the basics, yet there is so much more to know. But if your kids live by these five principles, they will be far and away better off financially than their peers.

> **DAD TIP:**
> *Credit card companies deluge our college-age children with preapproved cards (with large limits). Though it's not good to give kids free rein with credit, it's important that they learn to be responsible with purchases and to pay their cards off every month, which will build them a solid credit history.*

FIVE-TOOL SUCCESS

One's financial standing can be a significant measure of success, but there are several other dimensions of success that measure a person's true worth. Young adults and many parents tend to forget or fail to consider these other dimensions. Understanding that money and finances are just one aspect of success, you can help your children develop other viewpoints on what success really is.

In baseball, a "five-tool" player is one who can run, throw, field, hit for average, and hit with power. Few players fit the description of a five-tool player. When they do fulfill their potential in this way, they attain fame and fortune.

Highly successful people also have tools in five areas of success:

- **Financial Success:** Not necessarily having a lot of money, but knowing how to manage the money you do have.
- **Relationship Success:** Having loving friends and family members who can be counted on in good times and bad, just as they count on you.
- **Intellectual Success:** Maximizing your intellect by being open to others, their ideas, and their culture. Always being open to learning. Having confidence, patience, and empathy while understand-

ing your strengths and weaknesses, and those of others.

- **Physical Success:** Giving your body and mind the exercise, nutrients, and rest they need.
- **Spiritual Success:** Being able to live outside the needs of your ego with love and understanding for people and all living things.

> **DAD TIP:**
> *Being a "Five-Tool Success" isn't inborn; it's taught. And while both parents have a good deal to say in teaching this to their children, as Dads we can assess our children's abilities and objectively help them meet their goals.*

As fathers, giving our children these tools of success would be our own truest success. Look at each of your children. Which of these five tools does each of them need your help with? It will likely be different for each child. Spend time with each to teach, mentor, and encourage them as they make their way to success.

If you find one tool in which they *all* need help, it may be related to how they were raised. Hopefully you can recognize their shortcomings even if you have the same issues. To overcome these shortcomings, listen to the trusted advice of others, read voraciously, and practice what you learn. It will help if you can teach your children with the conviction of experience rather than just book learning.

IF YOU WANT *X*, YOU MUST *Y*

Years ago, I gave this list, mounted in one of those cheap plastic frames, to my three children. I'm sure they thought I was a nerdy dad. But they knew I cared for their future. Following this advice can help your children progress in each of the five aspects of success.

- If you want to **Learn**, you must **listen**.
- If you want **Growth**, you must **take risks**.

- If you want **Responsibility**, you must **be responsible**.
- If you want **Commitment**, you must **be involved**.
- If you want **Achievement**, you must **have goals**.
- If you want **Success**, you must **have persistence**.
- If you want **Control**, you must **plan**.
- If you want **Rewards**, you must **provide effort**.
- If you want to **Be Liked**, you must **like yourself**.
- If you want **Love**, you must **be patient**.
- If you want a **Challenge**, you must **dare to improve**.

Simply being told these lessons will not anchor them into your child's state of being. These lessons must be taught through example—concrete evidence of their efficacy, repeated multiple times.

Being a Dad is not checking things off a list to be sure you've covered it all. Being a Dad is being a teacher, a mentor, and an auditor, always evaluating your children's progress and life status. If you play these roles, the rewards will make it all more than worthwhile.

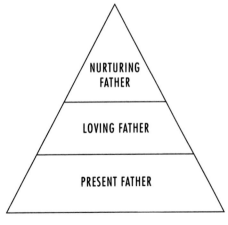

THE PYRAMID OF DADHOOD

YOUR ROAD MAP: CHAPTER 12

Start: Teach your children the value of money from a young age. Let them earn a small allowance through doing special chores around the house.

Major Highway: As your children grow, teaching them the importance of earning, saving, creating emergency funds, and planning for the future is vital for their financial comfort. Dads never stop teaching and mentoring in this area, even after their children are grown. It's a credit to your wise advice that they return with questions and seek your wisdom in financial as well as other matters as they mature.

On the Open Road: Helping your children use their money wisely and plan for the future, and teaching them to allow themselves to have fun with what they've earned, are both important. As with everything discussed in this book, balance is the key.

Twelfth Stop: Think about the principles under "If You Want *x*, You Must *y*." How many of these life lessons have your children learned? How many of them have you learned? What are your plans to help them (and possibly yourself) learn more?

CHAPTER 13

THE REWARDS AND A CONFESSION

"You are the best Daddy in the world."
—My older daughter at five years old

Like most people, I have had some awards and rewards in my life. I've overcome some obstacles that for others were roadblocks. I achieved my childhood goal of becoming an Air Force pilot, despite the concerns of many of my relatives who thought I would never make it because of my circumstances and family history. But what do I hold as the greatest achievement and reward of my life, never to be outdone? The love, success, and happiness of my children! Ask any mother and father of happy, successful children, and they all will most certainly feel this way.

YOU EARN YOUR KEEP

Parenting, being a good Dad, is hard work. Personal sacrifices are often necessary. There are times of frustration and disappointment. It sounds a lot like a job, doesn't it? But the rewards are so sweet, the memories are so wonderful, and the results are worth every sacrifice. The eyes that open wide when you enter a room, the smiles on your children's faces when they are happy, and the hugs they want from you when they need comforting—all beget mini bursts of adrenaline that keep you energized through the difficult periods.

Doing good for others will come back to you, especially when it involves your children. What you give your children in building their confidence and strengths minimizes your need to worry or intervene in their lives as they mature. You proudly display their artwork made especially for you, and you attend the recitals, ball games, and school plays—all performed wanting to please you and Mom. You live with their struggles and revel when they overcome them. As they grow more independent, you marvel at what they can accomplish and how they develop into independent and strong citizens. They can do this, in large part, because of you, their Dad.

MESSAGES OF LOVE

One morning before I started writing, my wife, Kathy, was cleaning out some drawers. It must have been a while since the last purge, because she found something April had hand made for me for my birthday many years ago. Judging by her handwriting, she must have been ten to twelve years old. It was a message on an eight-by-eleven-inch piece of paper creatively folded four times.

Before I unfolded it, I read a single word on the cover: "you"

I opened the first fold and it had "just don't know"

Then the second fold: "how wonderful, sensitive, caring, and understanding"

And the third: "of a daddy you are."

On the last fold, she wrote, "Happy Birthday—I love you more than you could ever know. Love, April."

I hadn't seen this birthday message in at least fifteen years and had forgotten about it. Every dirty diaper, sleepless night, instance of teenage backtalk, college expense, and endless night of worry and fear was repaid hundreds of times with the simple rereading of this gift.

In yet another drawer was a note from Rachel, written in a young girl's newly learned cursive, when she was about seven to nine years old. She wrote:

> XOXOXO My dad is nice and he will never be mean. I love him and I will never stop loving him. Love, Rachel

Wow! I can't think of anything I have ever received that could match those or any of my kids' notes. Not a promotion, raise, award, or any other type of recognition. Please know that these personal messages are not my way of proving what a great dad I am; they are simply examples of the heartwarming notes you will receive as a loving and responsible father.

ACTS OF LOVE

My son was not much for writing notes, but he rewarded me in so many ways. As a little boy, he always followed me around as I mowed the lawn or fixed things around the house. He wanted to help me in whatever I did.

He started college as an engineer because I did. He joined the Air Force ROTC because I did. He wanted to be a pilot because I was one. I knew he made many of his decisions because he respected me or wanted to make me proud of him. I knew that some of his decisions were not right for him, and he later corrected those on his own. He did finish college, but not in engineering, and he is currently an Army helicopter pilot, not an Air Force fixed-wing pilot. He still occasionally calls me for advice, and I hope he does until the day he knows more than I do. It won't be long now.

These are just a few examples of the many acts of love our children have shown their mom and me. We are proud of our children and appreciate their acts of love, but of course most families have wonderful and touching stories of their children. If you are a new father, you need to know what you have to look forward to. If you are an uninvolved father, you need to know what you have been missing and to take steps to turn that around.

THEY DON'T FORGET

Rachel was twenty-three years old when she wrote this short letter to me:

> Dear Dad,
>
> I remember . . .
>
> Leaving for family vacations early in the morning and sleeping for the first couple of hours . . .
>
> Then, being the first in the family to wake up, making eye contact with you in the rearview mirror, seeing you smile through your eyes—and then being thrown a York Peppermint Patty. I remember the look, the faint sound of the radio, and then the York being pulled from the bag. No words.
>
> Thank you for that.
>
> I love you,
>
> Rachel

April was thirty years old when she told me she remembered how I used to stroke her forehead and hair while she cuddled in my lap. Her mother did the same, and it made her feel so comforted and content. She reminded me of this when I was helping her get up and down while she had a pinched nerve in her back. It brought back her good memories of being cared for and loved, memories all children should have.

The memories April and Rachel recalled to me were not huge events, but simple, happy memories. They came from a connection filled with love: the kind of love that all children, and parents, need so much. Today and forever, what always brings a lump to my throat and tears to my eyes is the love I feel for, and get from, my son and two daughters. I am truly complete because of that, no matter how satisfying my professional life has been or will be.

SUBTLE REWARDS

Some rewards are so subtle, you won't even be aware of them if you don't take the time to look for them. My kids have the luxury of not needing constant contact with me, nor do I need to seek their attention. They are doing what I always wanted for them—happily living their lives. In no way are we avoiding each other. They know I am there for them and love them. Nothing need be proven—everything is natural. I know without a single doubt that they would be there for me no matter what, why, when, or how. When your children are adults, you no longer want them to *need* you in their lives; you want them to *want* you in their lives.

Be a good Dad to your children and your rewards will make you feel like you didn't do enough to deserve them. This is a promise.

CONFESSION

I was not a perfect father when my children were young. I didn't do everything I mention in this book because I learned some of the lessons too late for their benefit. I made mistakes and bad choices often. However, I was there for them physically and emotionally, I loved them openly, and I taught them what I knew at the time would help them grow into valued adults. This is the power of Dadhood. This, in a nutshell, is all you need to do to potentially save a life from unnecessary hardships. The answers are relatively easy; it's the execution that can be difficult.

PREVENTION, NOT REPARATION

Some fathers and mothers will have serious parenting issues to deal with as they raise their children. I haven't focused on how to fix the most serious issues but instead looked into ways to prevent those issues from arising. Never expect parenting to be a breeze. Challenges will confront you frequently, but you can be the antidote to the poisons that exist in our society.

Nor have I discussed in depth the current technologies that impact our children's lives: cell phones, cable television, computers, the Internet, and so on. These conveniences help us in our everyday lives, but they also bring more challenges in protecting our children from predators, immorality, misinformation, and so many influences that may counter our beliefs and the good of our children. But the answers to good parenting remain constant through all technological changes.

Absent or ineffective fathering is not a new phenomenon. There was no golden age of father-child connection to my knowledge. We may be fooled by television of the 1950s and 1960s where *Father Knows Best*, *Leave It to Beaver*, and *The Andy Griffith Show* showcased concerned, involved fathers. Mostly those TV shows were great examples of parenting, although maybe a little too idyllic to identify with for most of us. I was born in 1950 and lived a much less idyllic life, and I knew many others who did the same. There were also successful families then as there are now, at least in terms of staying together. We can't blame the times, nor can we blame technology or society for the ills of our own children. Those challenges can be overcome when fatherhood and motherhood are properly in place and working for our children.

TAKE THE CHALLENGE

"Patience is bitter, but its fruit is sweet."

—Aristotle

There is a depth to knowledge. You can agree with or understand a thought or idea logically, but not until you know it deeply in your heart through constant practice and attention will it change you. Know deeply your influence as a father. The light of knowledge can shine on you, but until that light penetrates you, there is no way to let it shine through to your children. Knowing *what* you can do as a father gives you the challenge. Knowing *how* to do it gives you the tools. But this knowledge is worthless without preparation, perspiration, and imagination. Let's help society, one kid at a time. Each kid will have the advantages of living in a healthy family and have children more likely to create a healthy family themselves. Healthy families together create safe and harboring neighborhoods, enriching communities, strong nations. Great societies do not exist without contributing citizens, and each child is a necessary building block to a great society.

Mold your children with love and intelligence, and do it early. Give them tools, not Band-Aids. Pay attention to their needs, correct their misperceptions, and give them a helping hand, not a handout. You can do it and you must. Everything I have suggested in this book is worthless to you without your best efforts as a father to practice these principles. Be the best Dad your children could ever have. You are the only man in the world who can do so.

ON YOUR OWN, BUT NOT ALONE

You are the only true father your children will ever have, but you are not alone. Your children are waiting for you. Their mother is longing for your help. Society is cheering for your success. Fathers who are true Dads are always ready to talk to you. And you've read this book—you're doing a bang-up job already!

> *"In lieu of flowers and contributions, Mr. McGrath requests that you go outside and play catch with a kid."*
> —Obituary of Francis B. McGrath Jr. of Jefferson County, Missouri,
> March 2010

YOUR ROAD MAP:
FOR THE REST OF THE JOURNEY

Dads, you have the right map, compass, and tools to guide your children through the impressionable years of their lives. Within you is the inspiration, the teaching skills, the patience, the wisdom, and the comforting they need. It is *you* they need: your love, your ear, your arms, your words. Unfold your map with courage, and journey onward.

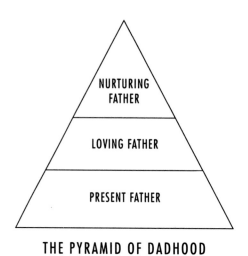

THE PYRAMID OF DADHOOD

THE SEVEN CHARACTERISTICS OF A SUCCESSFUL DAD

A SUCCESSFUL DAD WILL BE:

INVOLVED	PRINCIPLED	CONSISTENT	LOVING	FUN

PASSIONATE

BALANCED

As we have all witnessed, being a successful father is not an easy task! It's complicated because you'll find yourself asking, "What are the answers?" when the answers are unique to every dad and every child. Instead of answers, you can best rely on developing proven characteristics that, in one form or another, we have discussed in this book.

Although there are many, below are the characteristics I believe are the most important in being the best dad you can be. But none of these characteristics alone are sufficient, and sometimes not even beneficial, if not balanced with other important characteristics.

Be Involved. Be involved from the moment of your children's births. You are a parent, not a figurehead. Be there for important events. Be available when they need support. Be strong for them when they are afraid. Be careful to consider your children when you prioritize your life events. Be a listener!

Be Principled. You are being watched by your children. They assume you are the model they should follow. You must have personal values that will guide them in the right direction. Be honest. Be moral. Be sure you have rules and limits.

Be Consistent. Be reliable. Be a rock. Do what you say and say what you'll do. When you set goals and limits for your children, there should be rewards and consequences reinforcing them, as appropriate. If you're not consistent with your children, you will confuse them. Explain the reasons and situations that may require you to relax or tighten the rules. This keeps your children involved and informed, and avoids misunderstandings.

Be Loving. Be gentle. Be kind. Be understanding. Be protective. Give hugs and pats on the back. Give them your complete attention on occasion—especially when they need it. Sympathize when appropriate but show your concerns about improper behavior. That is also love.

Be Fun. Be a jokester, but don't force it. Surprise your children with occasional treats and adventures. Smile. Do crazy things—like balancing a broom on your nose. Play catch. Pretend with them. Have a tea party. Tease them in a kind, not demeaning, way. Know and be kind to their friends.

Be Balanced. The glue that makes all the other "be"s work is to be balanced. Be involved but not too involved. Be principled but don't be preachy. Be consistent but not inflexible. Be loving, but don't be a pushover. Be fun but be respected. Know your own limits. You cannot be consistent if you don't have principles. You can't be loving or fun if you are not involved.

Be Passionate. Being passionate about being a dad comes naturally to some men—but not to all. If you don't have a natural passion for fatherhood, then be passionate about reviewing this list of characteristics and thinking about how you can apply them. A father that has to work at being a dad can be a bigger hero for his children than those for which fathering comes easily.

A DAD'S
SELF-INSPECTION
CHECKLIST

I was in the military for twenty-nine years and a father for twenty-five of those years. In the military, we were constantly inspected by our superiors against strict standards. To be ready for these inspections, and to ensure that we were in compliance, we developed "self-inspection" checklists. Now that I write about fatherhood, I thought, why not have a self-inspection checklist for fathers? Often, we don't really know or think about what it is we could improve upon as dads. While you are not likely to be inspected on your parenting skills, you do want to be the best dad possible.

But are you the best dad you can be?

Following is a self-inspection checklist for dads. The questions are not intended to judge but to allow you to reflect on your relationship with your children. While some of the questions seem similar, they are reworded in ways that may apply better to your situation.

Be honest! Be reflective. Don't think you are a bad dad if you can't answer all these questions positively. There is no grade. This is just a vehicle to become a better dad. By the end of the checklist, you will be beaming, taking note of needed corrections, or, most likely, both.

A DAD'S SELF-INSPECTION CHECKLIST

ARE YOU *THERE* FOR YOUR CHILDREN, NOT JUST AROUND?

- Do you/did you hold your children as babies and toddlers?
- Do you enjoy spending time with your kids?
- Do you make time to focus on your kids?
- Would you consider yourself loving, and do your kids *know* that you care for them?
- On occasion, do you give your kids special one-on-one attention?
- Do you comfort your kids when appropriate?
- Are you willing to be "hated" for doing the right thing for your children?
- Do you really listen when spoken to?
- Do you and your children have fun together?

DO YOU HELP YOUR CHILDREN FACE THEIR FEARS?

- Do you push (encourage) your meek children forward and hold back (protect) your adventurous children?
- Are you aware of any peer pressure they may be facing and how to deal with it?
- Do you give them reachable challenges to conquer to build up their confidence?
- Do you praise their efforts and rejoice when they are persistent?
- Can you tell if and when your help will make them stronger or weaker?

DOES YOUR FAMILY WORK TOGETHER AND SUPPORT EACH OTHER?

- Do you and their mother see eye to eye on how to raise your children? Can you compromise?
- Do you continue to parent the only way you know how, or do you research other options?
- Are you aware of how much you, as a father, can influence your children in both positive and negative ways? If not, read my book or blog (http://www.michaelbyronsmith.com) on fatherhood.
- Do you develop family traditions that are loved by the entire family?
- Do you know your children's friends? Do you approve of their values?
- Is diversity allowed and cooperation encouraged in your home?
- Are you careful to not favor one child over another?
- Do you never give in, give in too much, or give in as appropriate to your children's requests?
- Do you communicate clearly with the children's mother regarding punishments, rewards, their whereabouts, schedule, and so forth?

ARE YOU A GOOD EXAMPLE TO YOUR CHILDREN, AND DO YOU REPRESENT YOURSELF WELL?

- Are you careful to not abuse your power as a father, using influence instead of force?
- Do you have an open mind toward things you don't understand?
- Are you consistent in your actions, discipline, encouragement, and love?
- Following your lead, are your children respectful and kind to others?
- Are you a good model for your daughters to know how to be treated by boys and other men?

IS BUILDING THE CHARACTER OF YOUR CHILDREN A CONSCIOUS PART OF YOUR PARENTING?

- Would you want your children to act as you do? Children will usually mimic you.
- Do you encourage your children's passions, dreams, and individuality?
- Do you realize that lessons taught when your children are young will be anchored in them, but missed lessons may haunt you for a long time? Prevention is much easier than healing!
- Do you allow them to make mistakes (for learning) when no one or nothing will get hurt?
- Do you teach or exemplify to your kids kindness, values, discipline, and manners?
- Do you praise good behavior while redirecting and correcting inappropriate behavior?
- Do you help them to make responsible choices?
- Do you tell your children mistakes are okay, but known wrongdoing is *not* a mistake?
- Do you instill integrity, teaching what's right to do and what's wrong to do?
- Do they know what humility means and how it can help them to be liked and respected?
- Do you teach your children to be self-reliant and responsible for their actions?
- Have you taught them how to earn, value, save, and spend money?
- Do your children know how to set and meet goals?
- Do you emphasize and support education?

If you have plowed through this checklist, congratulations! The mere fact that you went through it all indicates you probably did well on your self-inspection. Your most important personal contribution to your family and society is your dedication to the welfare of your children. But none of us are perfect, and we do have many distractions. It's good to review this checklist occasionally, perhaps every Father's Day week, to check up on yourself while you are checking up on your children. Ask for guidance if you could use some help!

BIBLIOGRAPHY

CHAPTER 1

"Appreciating How Fathers Give Children a Head Start." (NCPFCE) National Center on Parent, Family, and Community Engagement. Head Start: An Office of the Administration for Children and Families, Early Childhood Learning & Knowledge Center (ECLKC). Last modified September 15, 2014. http://eclkc.ohs.acf.hhs.gov/hslc/tta-system/family/for-families/Everyday%20Parenting/Fatherhood/parent_pub_00001_072005.html.

Princess. "Life of a Girl Who Needs Fatherly Love." Nairaland Forum. Posted September 24, 2005. http://www.nairaland.com/nigeria/topic-1488.0.html (site discontinued).

CHAPTER 2

Blankenhorn, David. *Fatherless America: Confronting Our Most Urgent Social Problem*. New York: Harper Perennial, 1995.

Coles, Robert. *The Moral Intelligence of Children: How to Raise a Moral Child*. New York: Penguin Group, 1997.

Pruett, Kyle D. "How Men and Children Affect Each Other's Development." *Zero to Three* 18, no. 1 (1997): 3–11.

CHAPTER 3

Hax, Carolyn. "Husband is willing to father baby but wouldn't interact with it." Tell Me About It. *Washington Post*, July 2, 2006. http://www.washingtonpost.com/wp-dyn/content/article/2006/06/29/AR2006062901860.html.

CHAPTER 4

Beck, Allen J., Susan A. Kline, and Lawrence A. Greenfield. *Survey of Youth in Custody, 1987*. Washington, DC: United States Department of Justice, Bureau of Justice Statistics, 1988. http://www.bjs.gov/content/pub/pdf/syc87.pdf.

Blankenhorn, David. *Fatherless America: Confronting Our Most Urgent Social Problem*. New York: Harper Perennial, 1995.

Bureau of the Census, as cited in Robert O'Block. "Roots of Uncertainty." *Annals of Psychotherapy and Integrative Health* (2008). http://www.annalsofpsychotherapy.com/articles/spring08.php?topic=article9.

(CDC) Center for Disease Control, as cited in Robert O'Block. "Roots of Uncertainty." *Annals of Psychotherapy and Integrative Health* (2008). http://www.annalsofpsychotherapy.com/articles/spring08.php?topic=article9.

Cornell, Dewey G., Elissa P. Benedek, and David M. Benedek. "Characteristics of Adolescents Charged with Homicide: Review of 72 Cases." *Behavioral Sciences and the Law* 5, no. 1 (1987): 11–23.

Ellis, Bruce J., John E. Bates, Kenneth A. Dodge, David M. Fergusson, L. John Horwood, Gregory S. Pettit, and Lianne Woodward. "Does Father Absence Place Daughters at Special Risk for Early Sexual Activity and Teenage Pregnancy?" *Child Development* 74, no. 3 (2003): 801–21.

Eyre, Richard and Linda Eyre. *The Turning*. Sanger, CA: Familius, 2014.

Farley, Maggie. "U.S., Britain Place Last in Child Survey." *Los Angeles Times*, February 15, 2007. http://articles.latimes.com/2007/feb/15/world/fg-children15.

Fathers Unite. "Fatherless Homes Now Proven Beyond Doubt Harmful to Children." Fathers Unite. Accessed September 13, 2014. http://fathersunite.org/statistics_on_fatherlessnes.html.

Knight, Raymond A. and Robert A. Prentky. "The Developmental An-
tecedents and Adult Adaptations of Rapist Subtypes." *Criminal
Justice and Behavior* 14, no. 4 (1987): 403–26.

Literallyamerican, November 5, 2011 (10:20 a.m.). Comment on Meg Mirshak. "Poor Parenting Leads Youth to
Violent Crime." *The Augusta Chronicle*, November 5, 2011.
http://chronicle.augusta.com/news/crime-courts/2011-11-05/
poor-parenting-leads-youth-violent-crime.

McCullough, David, Jr. "You Are Not Special." Filmed June 1, 2012.
Wellesley Media Corporation video, 12:45. Posted June 7, 2012,
http://youtu.be/_lfxYhtf8o4.

(NFI) National Fatherhood Initiative. *Father Facts*. 6th ed. 2011.

O'Neill, Rebecca. "Experiments in Living: The Fatherless Family." *Civi-
tas: The Institute for the Study of Civil Society*. (2002), http://www.
civitas.org.uk/pubs/experiments.php.

Pittman, Frank. *Man Enough: Fathers, Sons, and the Search for Masculinity*. New York: Perigee Books, 1993.

Pressfield, Steven. *The War of Art: Break Through the Blocks and Win
Your Inner Creative Battles*. New York: Black Irish Entertainment,
2012.

Sedlak, Andrea J. and Diane D. Broadhurst. *Third National Incidence
Study of Child Abuse and Neglect*. Washington, DC: U.S. Department of Health and Human Services, 1996.

Strand, Mark. Quoted from interview in Mihaly Csikszentmihalyi.
Creativity: Flow and the Psychology of Discovery and Invention.
New York: HarperCollins, 1996.

UNICEF. "Child Poverty in Perspective: An Overview of Child
Well-Being in Rich Countries." *Innocenti Report Card* 7 (2007).

CHAPTER 5

Pressfield, Steven. *The War of Art: Break Through the Blocks and Win
Your Inner Creative Battles*. New York: Black Irish Entertainment,
2012.

CHAPTER 6

Braver, Sanford H., Sharlene A. Wolchik, Irwin N. Sandler, Bruce S. Fogas, and Daria Zvetina. "Frequency of Visitation by Divorced Fathers: Differences in Reports by Fathers and Mothers." *American Journal of Orthopsychiatry* 61, no. 3 (1991): 448–54.

Bryan, Mark. *The Prodigal Father: Reuniting Fathers and Their Children.* New York: Random House, 1997.

Diamond, John. *Life Energy: Using the Meridians to Unlock the Hidden Power of Your Emotions.* New York: Paragon House, 1985.

O'Connell, Mark. *The Good Father: On Men, Masculinity, and Life in the Family.* New York: Scribner, 2005.

Pittman, Frank. *Man Enough: Fathers, Sons, and the Search for Masculinity.* New York: Perigee Books, 1993.

CHAPTER 7

(NFI) National Fatherhood Initiative. *Father Facts.* 6th ed. 2011.

Popenoe, David. *Life Without Father: Compelling New Evidence That Fatherhood and Marriage Are Indispensable for the Good of Children and Society.* New York: Free Press, 1996.

Swift, Madelyn. *Discipline for Life: Getting It Right with Children.* Southlake, TX: Childright, 1999.

CHAPTER 8

Ahern, Laurie and Eric Rosenthal. *Hidden Suffering: Romania's Segregation and Abuse of Infants and Children with Disabilities.* Washington, DC: Mental Disability Rights International, 2006.

Kerckhoff, Andy. *Critical Connection: A Practical Guide to Parenting Young Teens.* Cape Girardeau, MO: White Orchard Press, 2013.

Maeroff, Gene I. *Building Blocks: Making Children Successful in the Early Years of School.* New York: Palgrave Macmillan, 2006.

Pittman, Frank. *Man Enough: Fathers, Sons, and the Search for Masculinity.* New York: Perigee Books, 1993.

Pruett, Kyle D. "How Men and Children Affect Each Other's Development." *Zero to Three* 18, no. 1 (1997): 3–11.

Russert, Tim. *Wisdom of Our Fathers: Lessons and Letters from Daughters and Sons*. New York: Random House, 2006.

"The Shame of a Nation." YouTube video, 54:23. Uploaded June 30, 2014, by user "Zammie1170." From an episode of *20/20* on ABC News. http://youtu.be/HHY19ey2eDc.

CHAPTER 9

Csikszentmihalyi, Mihaly. *The Evolving Self: A Psychology for the Third Millennium*. New York: HarperCollins, 1993.

L'Estrange, Roger. *Fables of Aesop and Other Eminent Mythologists: with Morals and Reflections*. London: 1692.

CHAPTER 10

Coles, Robert. *The Moral Intelligence of Children: How to Raise a Moral Child*. New York: Penguin Group, 1997.

Mihaly Csikszentmihalyi. *Creativity: Flow and the Psychology of Discovery and Invention*. New York: HarperCollins, 1996.

CHAPTER 11

Hutchinson, Earl Ofari. *Black Fatherhood: The Guide to Male Parenting*. Manassas Park, VA: IMPACT! Publications, 1992.

Kalter, Neil. "Long-Term Effects of Divorce on Children: A Developmental Vulnerability Model." *American Journal of Orthopsychiatry* 57, no. 4 (1987): 587–600.

Meeker, Meg. *Strong Fathers, Strong Daughters: 10 Secrets Every Father Should Know*. New York: Ballantine Books, 2007.

Moehringer, J. R. *The Tender Bar: A Memoir*. New York: Hyperion, 2005.

O'Connell, Mark. *The Good Father: On Men, Masculinity, and Life in the Family*. New York: Scribner, 2005.

Pittman, Frank. *Man Enough: Fathers, Sons, and the Search for Masculinity*. New York: Perigee Books, 1993.

CHAPTER 12

Kiyosaki, Robert T. *Rich Dad, Poor Dad for Teens: The Secrets about Money That You Don't Learn in School!* New York: Warner Books and Little, Brown and Company, 2004.

ABOUT THE AUTHOR

Michael Byron Smith is a retired military officer and civilian engineer. He has been married for forty years and has three children and four grandchildren. He lives in Ballwin, Missouri, and loves being a father and grandfather.

ABOUT FAMILIUS

Welcome to a place where mothers and fathers are celebrated, not belittled. Where values are at the core of happy family life. Where boo boos are still kissed, cake beaters are still licked, and mistakes are still okay. Welcome to a place where books—and family—are beautiful. Familius: a book publisher dedicated to helping families be happy.

VISIT OUR WEBSITE: WWW.FAMILIUS.COM

Our website is a different kind of place. Get inspired, read articles, discover books, watch videos, connect with our family experts, download books and apps and audiobooks, and along the way, discover how values and happy family life go together.

JOIN OUR FAMILY

There are lots of ways to connect with us! Subscribe to our newsletters at www.familius.com to receive uplifting daily inspiration, essays from our Pater Familius, a free ebook every month, and the first word on special discounts and Familius news.

BECOME AN EXPERT

Familius authors and other established writers interested in helping families be happy are invited to join our family and contribute online content. If you have something important to say on the family, join our expert community by applying at:

www.familius.com/apply-to-become-a-familius-expert

GET BULK DISCOUNTS

If you feel a few friends and family might benefit from what you've read, let us know and we'll be happy to provide you with quantity discounts. Simply email us at specialorders@familius.com.

Website: www.familius.com
Facebook: www.facebook.com/paterfamilius
Twitter: @familiustalk, @paterfamilius1
Pinterest: www.pinterest.com/familius

The most important work you ever

do will be within the walls of your

own home.

Lightning Source UK Ltd.
Milton Keynes UK
UKOW04f0341021015

259683UK00003B/37/P